L Wilcnunshi

Quick Reference Guide

Microsoft®
Word 97

Don Mayo & Cathy Vesecky

275 Madison Ave., NY 10016
http://www.ddcpub.com

ABOUT THIS GUIDE

This manual provides quick and thorough instructions for essential operations used in Word 97 for Windows. Simple step–by–step directions lead you through both mouse and keyboard procedures for each task, making it quick and easy to accomplish what you need to.

For exercises and instruction on Word, refer to DDC's Learning Word 97 for Windows. *For more information on Windows operating systems, refer to DDC's* Learning Windows 95 *or* Microsoft Office 97 Quick Reference Guide.

Authors: **Don Mayo & Cathy Vesecky**
Managing Editor: **Kathy Berkemeyer**
English Editor: **Cathy Vesecky**
Technical Editor: **Cathy Vesecky**
Layout: **Cathy Vesecky**

I would like to thank Cathy Vesecky, Jennifer Frew, Peter McCarthy, my family and friends, Kathy Berkemeyer, and, as always, John Visaggi. –Don Mayo

ii   Table of Contents

Table of Contents   iii

iv   Table of Contents

Table of Contents   v

vi   Table of Contents

Table of Contents

viii   Table of Contents

Table of Contents ix

x   Table of Contents

INTRODUCTION

WHAT THIS MANUAL COVERS

The 11 sections in this manual are broken down as follows:

Introduction
Explains how this manual works.

Screen Elements
Defines basic screen elements in Word 97.

Basics
Covers basic skills for navigating through Word and manipulating text and objects, including copying and pasting text, resizing windows, moving the cursor, and accessing help.

Manage Files
Explains how to work with files. Opening, closing, and saving, for example, are covered here.

View Options
Covers the on–screen display options available in Word.

Format/Edit
Contains information on the various ways of formatting and editing information in a document.

Pictures and Other Objects
Explains how to create, insert, format, and edit objects, such as Clip Art and AutoShapes, in a Word document.

Tables
Explains how to create and format tables in a Word document.

continued...

References

Explains how to reference information, such as footnotes, indexes, and tables of contents, in a Word document.

Proofing and Review Tools

Explains how to use proofing and review tools in Word, including the spell and grammar check, comments, and revision marks.

Mail Options

Explains how to create a mail merge, as well as how to create envelopes and labels.

CONVENTIONS

Command Examples

Procedures in this guide are generally composed of a series of numbered steps. To complete a procedure, it is necessary to complete the steps in sequential order. As shown in the example below, you usually have a choice of both mouse and keyboard methods of completing a step. In many instances, these methods are combined, as in the following example:

1.   Click **File** menu... Alt + F

This step indicates that you can access the File menu either by clicking on its name in the menu bar, or by holding down the **Alt** key while pressing the **F** key.

continued.

In cases where multiple mouse and keystroke methods are shown for one task, the commands are either broken down into separate subheadings (e.g., *Copy Text Using Toolbar* and *Copy Text Using Menu*), or they are divided by the word *OR*, as below:

1. Click **File Open** button in **Standard** toolbar.

   OR

   Click **File, Open**.............................. `Alt`+`F`,`O`

   OR

   Press **Ctrl+O**.. `Ctrl`+`O`

As in the example above, mouse steps generally appear first, followed by the corresponding keystrokes. Keystroke shortcuts appear last.

Keystrokes are listed to the right of steps in reverse type (e.g., `Alt`+`F`). Although this manual lists these keyboard characters in uppercase letters, they should be typed as lowercase, unless accompanied by the **Shift** key, as in: `Alt`+`Shift`+`F`

When you see a substitution word to the right of a step, (e.g., *text*), type the required value, such as a file name or a measurement.

When selecting commands in Word dialog boxes, you can often activate them by double–clicking. Also, number settings can often be increased or decreased by clicking scroll arrows. Note that these procedures are not always illustrated in this manual.

continued...

xiv

In addition to the command procedures included in this Quick Reference Guide, other techniques for executing a given task often exist. The techniques listed here represent the easiest, most commonly used procedures.

Action Words

Four verbs are consistently used throughout this guide to indicate specific actions. You can:

Click a menu item or on–screen button.

Select an item from a drop–down list or a check box item in a dialog box, or select (highlight) text or graphics on screen.

Press a keyboard key.

Type information.

Units of Measurement

Since the default unit of measurement for most Word commands is inches, most measurements given in this manual are also in inches. However, different units of measurement can be typed in various dialog boxes, including points, picas, and centimeters. *(See **GENERAL OPTIONS**, page 14, for information on changing the default unit of measurement.)*

SCREEN ELEMENTS IN WORD 97

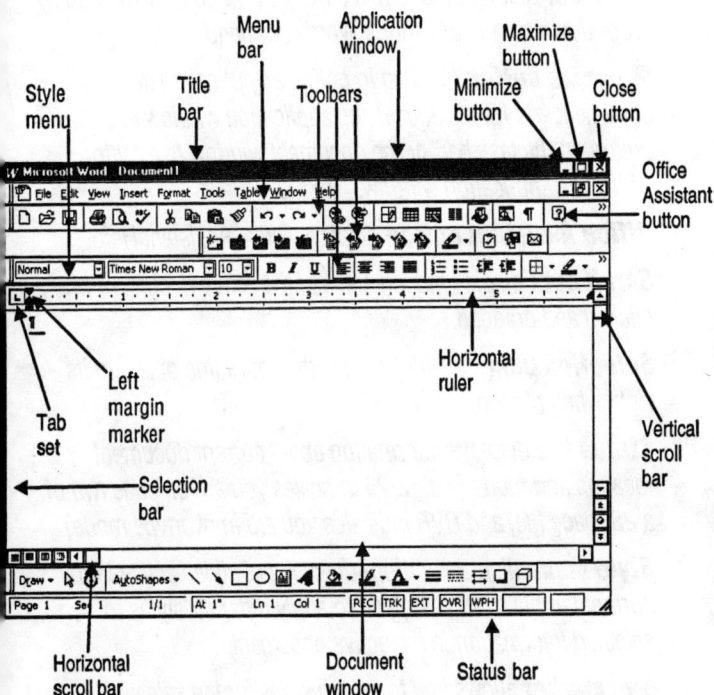

Application window *displays Word menus and toolbars, and contains the active document window(s).*

Close button *(located in both the application and the document windows) closes the active window.*

Document window *appears in and is restricted to the Word application window.*

Horizontal ruler *displays settings for selected paragraph.*

Margin markers *set margins for selected paragraph(s) when clicked and dragged along the horizontal ruler.*

Maximize button *(located in both the application and document windows) enlarges the application window to fill the screen, or the document window to fill the application window.*

continued

2

SCREEN ELEMENTS (CONTINUED)

Menu bar *displays menu names, which, when clicked, display drop–down menus of various Word commands.*

Minimize button *(located in both the application and document windows) reduces the application window to a button on the task bar, or the document window to a button within the application window.*

Office Assistant button *displays Office Assistant Help.*

Scroll bars *display hidden areas of the active document when clicked and dragged.*

Selection bar *(invisible) selects the entire line of text to its right when clicked.*

Status bar *displays information about current document location and mode (e.g., 2/25 indicates you are on page two of a 25–page file, and OVR indicates you are in overtype mode).*

Style menu *displays a drop–down list of styles active in the current template, allowing you to apply different styles to selected information in the active document.*

Tab marker *allows you to set tab stops for the selected paragraph by clicking on it until desired tab marker displays (left, right, center, or decimal) and then clicking on the horizontal ruler where you want to locate tab stop. You can reset tabs by dragging markers along the horizontal ruler.*

Title bar *displays the program name, and may display the name of the open file, if the document window is maximized. You can drag the title bar to move the window if the application window is not maximized.*

Toolbars *contain buttons that allow you to access Word commands quickly by clicking on them with the mouse. You can choose from the various default toolbars in Word or create your own. (See **TOOLBARS**, page 82. Also see your online **Help** for information on creating your own toolbar sets.)*

continued.

SHORTCUT MENUS

Many Word commands can be accessed quickly from
Shortcut Menus*. Shortcut menus contain commands*
generally related to the item you are working with and can be
*accessed by right–clicking the mouse or pressing **Shift+F10**.*
The menus appear in the document window next to your work
area, and available commands vary, depending on the selected
information.

Example of a Shortcut Menu:

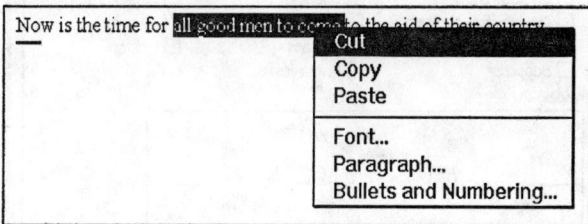

Now is the time for all good men to come to the aid of their country
Cut
Copy
Paste
Font...
Paragraph...
Bullets and Numbering...

PREVIEWS IN DIALOG BOXES

*Many dialog boxes in Word contain **Preview** boxes, which*
display a graphic representation of a particular selection, as it
*will look in your document. For example, the **Preview** box in*
*the **Font** dialog box displays an example of selected fonts,*
point sizes, and other style characteristics. (See next page.)

continued...

4

SCREEN ELEMENTS (CONTINUED)

Example of the Preview Box in the Fonts dialog box:

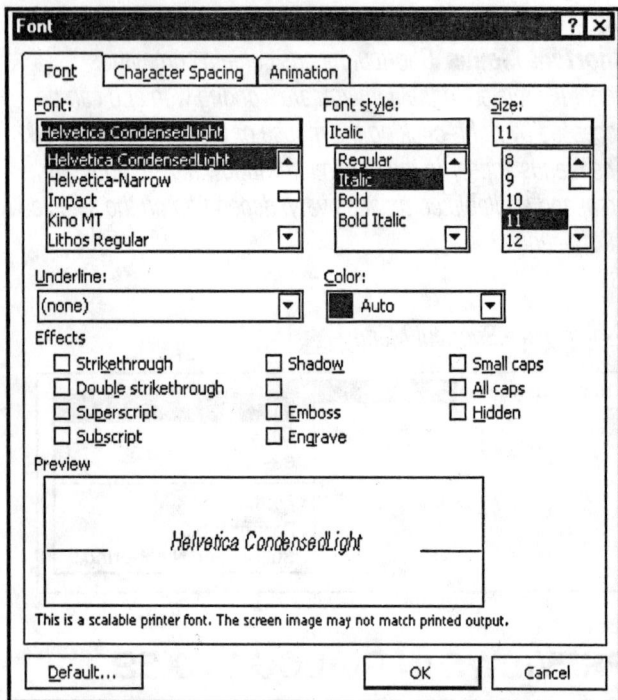

Font	? X

Font	Character Spacing	Animation

Font: Helvetica CondensedLight

Font style:	Italic

Size:	11

Helvetica CondensedLight
Helvetica-Narrow
Impact
Kino MT
Lithos Regular

Regular
Italic
Bold
Bold Italic

8
9
10
11
12

Underline: (none)

Color: Auto

Effects

☐ Strikethrough   ☐ Shadow   ☐ Small caps
☐ Double strikethrough   ☐   ☐ All caps
☐ Superscript   ☐ Emboss   ☐ Hidden
☐ Subscript   ☐ Engrave

Preview

_____ *Helvetica CondensedLight* _____

This is a scalable printer font. The screen image may not match printed output.

Default...   OK   Cancel

BASICS
COMPATIBILITY

*You can open documents created in earlier versions of Word, as well as in a number of other word–processing programs, in Word 97. Select how to display documents from other applications on the **Compatibility** tab under **Tools**, **Options**.*

> *Note: You cannot open a file created in Word 97 in earlier versions of Word.*

Display Compatibility

1. Click **Tools, Options** .... `Alt`+`T`,`O`

*The **Options** dialog box displays.*

2. Click | Compatibility |

3. Click **Recommended Options** .... `Alt`+`M`,`↑` `↓`
   For box and select program to
   set display options for from list.

4. Click **Options** list box .... `Alt`+`O`,`↑` `↓`
   and select display options.

   > *Note: Options only affect a document while you work on it in Word. They do not permanently change the file.*

   To use selected options as default settings for current document and all new documents based on current template:

   a. Click | **Default...** | .... `Alt`+`D`

   b. Click | **Yes** | .... `Alt`+`Y`
      when confirmation box appears.

5. Click | **OK** | .... `↵`

6

Font Substitution

Substitutes fonts used in active document that are not installed on your computer with resident fonts. This command substitutes fonts only while you are in Word; it does not permanently change them.

1. Click **Tools, Options** .... `Alt` + `T` , `O`

*The **Options** dialog box displays.*

2. Click `Compatibility`

3. Click `Font Substitution...` .... `Alt` + `S`

*If the current document contains fonts that are not installed on your computer, the **Font Substitution** dialog box displays.*

4. Click **Missing Document** .... `Alt` + `M` , `↑` `↓`
   Font box and select font to replace.

5. Click **Substituted font** box .... `Alt` + `S` , `↑` `↓`
   and select replacement font.

6. Repeat steps 4–5 for other fonts to substitute.

7. Click `Convert Permanently...` .... `Alt` + `P`
   if desired, to substitute fonts permanently.

8. Click `OK` twice .... `↵` , `↵`

COPY

*Copies information to the Clipboard. (See **PASTE**, page 28.)*

1. Select information to copy.

2. Click **Copy** button 📑 on **Standard** toolbar.
   OR
   Click **Edit, Copy** .... `Alt` + `E` , `C`
   OR
   Press **Ctrl+C** .... `Ctrl` + `C`

CUT

*Cuts (or moves) selected information to the Clipboard. (See **PASTE**, page 28.)*

1. Select information to cut.

2. Click **Cut** button 🔪 in **Standard** toolbar.

   OR

   Click **E**dit, Cu**t**.................................. `Alt`+`E`,`T`

   OR

   Press **Ctrl+X**.. `Ctrl`+`X`

DELETE

Deletes selected information from a document.

1. Select information to delete.

2. Click **E**dit, Cle**a**r.............................. `Alt`+`E`,`A`

   OR

   Press **Delete**... `Delete`

   OR

   Press **Backspace**.................................. `Backspace`

DOCUMENT WINDOWS
Arrange All

Arranges document windows next to each other on the screen.

Click **W**indow, **A**rrange All...................... `Alt`+`W`,`A`

8

Close Window

*(See also **CLOSE FILE**, page 38, or **Minimize Window**, page 9.)*

1. Click **Close** button ☒ in upper–right corner of active document window.

    OR

    a. Click **Control** menu button 🗗 in upper–left corner of active document window.

    b. Click **C**lose... Ⅽ

    OR

    Press **Ctrl+W** .... Ctrl + W

2. Click ⌊ Yes ⌉ .... Ⓨ
    to save document information.

    OR

    Click ⌊ No ⌉ .... Ⓝ
    to close window without saving.

Maximize Window

Enlarges active document window to fill application window.

> Note: This option is not available if window is already maximized.

Click **Maximize** button ❐ in upper–right corner of active document window.

OR

a. Click **Control** menu button 🗗 in upper–left corner of active document window.

b. Click Ma**x**imize... Ⅹ

OR

Press **Ctrl+F10** .... Ctrl + F10

Minimize Window

Reduces active document window to an icon bar on the bottom of the Word application screen.

Click **Minimize** button ⬚ in upper–right corner of active document window.

OR

a. Click **Control** menu button 🖾 in upper–left corner of active document window.

b. Click Mi<u>n</u>imize .... N

Move Window

> *Note:* A window cannot be moved if it is maximized or minimized. (See **Maximize Window**, page 8, or **Minimize Window**, above.)

MOVE WINDOW USING MOUSE

1. Place pointer on title bar of active window.

2. Click and drag window to desired position.

3. Release mouse button.

MOVE WINDOW USING CONTROL MENU

1. a. Click **Control** menu button 🖾 in upper–left corner of active document window.

   b. Click <u>M</u>ove .... M

   OR

   Press **Ctrl+F7** .... Ctrl + F7

The pointer changes to: ✥

2. Press arrow keys .... ↑ ↓ ← → to move border.

3. Press **ENTER** .... ↵ when window has reached desired position.

New Window

Opens a new window containing contents of active document.

> *Note:*   *Any editing or formatting performed in one window of a document is copied in all other windows of that document.*

Click **Window**, **New Window** .... `Alt`+`W`, `N`

Next Window

> *Note:*   *You can also choose a different document window by selecting the desired window from the bottom of the **Window** menu.*

Press **Ctrl+F6** .... `Ctrl`+`F6`

Resize Window

> *Note:*   *A window cannot be resized if it is maximized or minimized. (See **Maximize Window**, page 8, or **Minimize Window**, page 9.)*

RESIZE WINDOW USING MOUSE

1. Move pointer to side or corner of active document window until it changes to: ↔

2. Click and drag mouse until window reaches desired size.

3. Release mouse button.

RESIZE WINDOW USING CONTROL MENU

1. a. Click **Control** menu button 🗗 in upper–left corner of active document window.

    b. Click **Size** .... `S`

    OR

    Press **Ctrl+F8** .... `Ctrl`+`F8`

The pointer changes to: ✛

continued.

RESIZE WINDOW USING CONTROL MENU (CONTINUED)

2. Press arrow keys........................... ↑ ↓ ← →
    to move cursor to border of window to resize.

The pointer changes to: ↕

3. Click and drag mouse until window reaches desired size.

    OR

    a. Press arrow keys..................... ↑ ↓ ← →
        to move window border.

    b. Press **ENTER** .... ↵
        when window reaches desired size.

Restore Window

*Returns a minimized or maximized document window to standard size, so that it can be moved and resized. (See **Move Window**, page 9, and **Resize Window**, page 10.)*

Click **Restore window** button 🗗 in upper–right corner of maximized or minimized document window.

OR

a. Click **Control** menu button 🗗 in upper–left corner of maximized or minimized document window.

b. Click **Restore**.. R

OR

Press **Ctrl+F5**... Ctrl + F5

12

Split Window

Splits a document window into two panes, allowing you to view two different parts of the document simultaneously.

1. Click <u>W</u>indow, <u>S</u>plit .... `Alt`+`W`,`S`

The mouse pointer changes to ⇵ and is positioned in the middle of the screen on top of the split bar.

2. a. Drag mouse to move split bar.

   b. Click left mouse button when split bar reaches desired position.

   OR

   a. Press **Up** or **Down** arrow keys .... `↑` `↓` to move split to desired position.

   b. Press **ENTER**... `↵`

   To remove split:
   Double–click split bar separating the two windows.
   OR
   Click <u>W</u>indow, Remove <u>S</u>plit .... `Alt`+`W`,`S`

Move or Copy Text between Parts of a Document

1. Split document window. *(See **Split Window**, above.)*

2. Display information to move or copy in one pane.

3. Display the location where you want to move or copy the text or graphics in the other pane.

   To move information between panes:

   a. Select the text or graphics to move.

   b. Click and drag selected information across the split bar. *(See **DRAG AND DROP**, below.)*

continued.

MOVE/COPY TEXT BETWEEN PARTS OF DOCUMENT (CONT)

To copy information between panes:

a. Select text or graphics to copy.

b. Press and hold the **Control** key..................Ctrl
   while you click and drag selected information
   across the split bar.

c. Release the **Control** key and the mouse
   button when finished copying.

DRAG AND DROP

Note: *Drag–and–drop editing can be disabled*
*with the Edit tab under **Tools**, **Options**.*
(See EDIT OPTIONS, page 111.)

Move

1. Select information you want to move.

2. Click and drag selected information to new location.

Mouse changes to drag–and–drop pointer:

3. Position pointer where you want to insert
   information and release mouse button.

Copy

1. Select information you want to copy.

2. Press **Control** ....Ctrl
   while you click and drag selected
   information to new location.

Mouse changes to drag–and–drop pointer:

3. Position pointer where you want to copy the
   information and release mouse button.

14

EXIT WORD

Double–click application **Control menu** button 🔲 in upper–left corner of application window.

OR

Click **File**, E**x**it .... Alt + F , X

OR

Press **Alt+F4** .... Alt + F4

GENERAL OPTIONS

Enables/disables various Word features for global use.

1. Click **Tools**, **Options** .... Alt + T , O

*The **Options** dialog box displays.*

2. Click │ General │

3. Select from the following **General** options:

- **Background repagination** .... Alt + B
  to have Word automatically repaginate current document as you type/edit.

- **Help for WordPerfect users** .... Alt + W
  to have Word automatically display instructions or demonstrate how to perform a command in Word97 after you press its equivalent WordPerfect for DOS key combination.

- **Navigation keys for WordPerfect users** .... Alt + V
  to have Word change the default functions for the **Page Up**, **Page Down**, **Home**, **End**, and **Escape** keys to their WordPerfect for DOS equivalents.

- **Blue background, white text** .... Alt + U
  to set Word to display text in white on a blue background.

continued.

GENERAL OPTIONS (CONTINUED)

- **Provide feedback with sound** .... `Alt` + `S`
  to have sound automatically accompany
  various Word actions.

- **Provide feedback with animation** .... `Alt` + `N`
  to have animation automatically accompany
  various Word actions.

- **Confirm conversions at open** .... `Alt` + `O`
  to be able to manually select the converter
  for opening a document created in another
  application. Deselect this option to have Word
  select the correct converter automatically.

- **Update automatic links at open**............ `Alt` + `L`
  to have Word automatically update any
  information linked to other files every time
  you open a file.

- **Mail as attachment** .... `Alt` + `T`
  to have Word attach current document to
  an e–mail message, rather than inserting its
  contents into the e–mail message itself,
  when you click **File**, **Send to**, **Mail Recipient**.

- **Recently used file list** .... `Alt` + `R`
  to have Word automatically display the
  most recently opened documents at the
  bottom of the **File** menu.

  Click **entries** box .... `Alt` + `E`, *number*
  and type number of recently
  opened files to display.

- **Macro virus protection** .... `Alt` + `P`
  to have Word display a warning whenever you
  open a document that may contain macro viruses.

continued...

GENERAL OPTIONS (CONTINUED)

4. Click **Measurement units** box..... `Alt`+`M`,`↑``↓`
    and select a default measurement unit.

5. Click [OK]...................................... `↵`

HELP

Get Help from the Office Assistant

Microsoft Word Help is now administered by the Office Assistant, an animated character that offers an interactive approach to accessing help information.

1. Click the **Help** button 🔲 in the **Standard** toolbar.

    OR

    Click **Help, Microsoft Word Help**...... `Alt`+`H`,`H`

    OR

    Press **F1** .... `F1`

The Office Assistant appears with interactive help bubble:

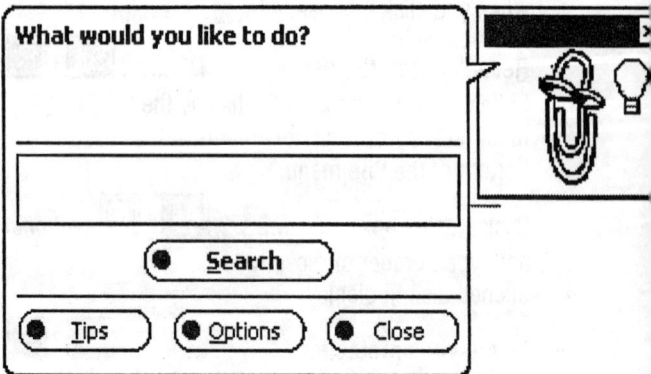

What would you like to do?

(● **Search**)

(● **Tips**) (● **Options**) (● **Close**)

continued

GET HELP FROM THE OFFICE ASSISTANT (CONTINUED)

2. Type in a question, keyword, or phrase concerning task/topic you need help with.

3. Click (● **Search**)

A list of related Help topics displays in the Office Assistant bubble.

4. Click desired topic.

Microsoft Word Help Topics *window opens, displaying information on selected topic and/or instructions for related tasks.*

To print topic:

a. Click [Options] .... O

b. Click **P**rint Topic .... P

The ***Print*** *dialog box displays.*

c. Select desired print options. *(See* ***PRINT****, page 29, and* ***Print Options****, page 31.)*

d. Click [OK] .... ↵

To go to Microsoft Word Help Contents and Index:

a. Click [Help **T**opics] .... T

(See ***Microsoft Word Help Contents****, page 20,* ***Microsoft Word Help Index****, page 21, and* ***Help Topics Find Feature****, page 21.)*

To hide Office Assistant:

Click **Close** button ☒ in upper–right corner of the Office Assistant character box.

HIDE OFFICE ASSISTANT AT STARTUP

When you start Word 97 for the first time, you must respond to the Office Assistant before you can use the program. Use this procedure to prevent this when you start the program in the future.

Click **Show these choices at startup** in the Office Assistant balloon to clear the check box.

SPECIFY WHEN OFFICE ASSISTANT AUTOMATICALLY APPEARS

The Office Assistant pops up on screen whenever you perform certain actions. Use this procedure to control when it appears.

1. Right–click in the Office Assistant window.

2. Click **Options** .... O
   from the submenu that appears.

3. Select options as desired to specify when Office Assistant will automatically appear.

   Note: *You can deselect all options if you never want the Assistant to appear automatically.*

4. Click OK .... ⏎

CHANGE OFFICE ASSISTANT CHARACTER

1. a. Right–click Office Assistant character.

   b. Click **Choose Assistant** C
      from shortcut menu that displays.

   OR

   a. Click **Office Assistant** button 🔳 in **Standard** toolbar.

   b. Click Options .... Alt + O

*The **Office Assistant** dialog box displays.*

2. Click Gallery .... Alt + G

continued..

CHANGE OFFICE ASSISTANT CHARACTER (CONTINUED)

3. Click [Next>] .... N

   OR

   Click [<Back] .... B

   to view **Office Assistant** options.

4. Click [OK] .... ⏎

   to select the Office Assistant character
   currently displayed and close the dialog box.

Get Help from the Help Menu

*The Help menu allows you to access help information from a
number of different sources, including Microsoft Word Help,
What's This? Help, Microsoft on the Web, WordPerfect Help,
and About Microsoft Word.*

1. Click **Help** menu .... Alt + H

   and select one of the following help sources:

   - **Microsoft Word Help** .... H
     to open the Office Assistant. *(See **Get Help
     from the Office Assistant**, page 16.)*

   - **Contents and Index** C
     to open the **Help Topics** dialog box and search
     its index or contents, or to use its Find feature.
     *(See **Microsoft Word Help Contents**, page 20,
     Microsoft Word Help Index, page 21, **Help Topics
     Find Feature**, page 21.)*

   - **What's This?** .... T
     to change mouse pointer to: ▶? which displays
     information boxes when clicked on screen items.
     *(See **What's This?**, page 25.)*

20

- Microsoft on the <u>W</u>eb .... W
  to connect to Microsoft Internet sites.
  (See Microsoft on the Web, page 22.)

- Word<u>P</u>erfect Help .... P
  to get help performing WordPerfect tasks in
  Word 97. *(See WordPerfect Help, page 23.)*

- <u>A</u>bout Microsoft Word .... A
  to display software, system, and technical
  support information. *(See About Microsoft
  Word, page 24.)*

MICROSOFT WORD HELP CONTENTS

1. Click <u>H</u>elp, <u>C</u>ontents and Index ...... Alt + H , C

   The Help Topics dialog box displays.

2. Click Contents

3. Click book icon ● next to desired topic.

4. Click Open .... Alt + O

   Subtopics display below original topic.

5. Click question mark ? next to desired subtopic.

6. Click Display .... Alt + D

   *The Microsoft Word Help Topics dialog box appears,
   displaying help information on selected topic.*

Microsoft Word Help Index

1. Click **H**elp, **C**ontents and Index........ `Alt`+`H`,`C`

2. Click `Index`

3. Click the **T**ype the first few letters..... `Alt`+`T`, *text*
   of the word you're looking for box and
   type the first letters of desired topic.

   OR

   Click the **C**lick the index entry....... `Alt`+`C`,`↑``↓`
   you want box and select topic from list.

4. Click `Display` .... `Alt`+`D`

*The **Microsoft Word Help Topics** dialog box appears,
displaying help information on selected topic.*

Help Topics Find Feature

1. Click **H**elp, **C**ontents and Index .... `Alt`+`H`,`C`

2. Click `Find`

3. Click the **T**ype the word(s)............. `Alt`+`T`,`↑``↓`
   you want to find box and type
   keyword or category associated
   with topic to look up.

*Word searches the entire contents of its Help database and
displays matching words in the **Select some words to
narrow your search** box, and matching topics in the **Click
a topic** box.*

continued...

22

4. Click the **Select some words** .... `Alt` + `S` , `↑` `↓`
   to narrow your search box and
   select desired words to narrow search by.

   Note: *To select a series of adjacent words from*
   the list, click on first word to select, then
   *press **Shift** and click on last word to select*
   in series. To select a number of
   nonadjacent words, click on first word to
   *select, then press **Control** and click on*
   each additional word to select.

5. Click the **Click a topic** box .... `Alt` + `C` , `↑` `↓`
   and select desired topic to look up.

6. Click `Display` .... `Alt` + `D`

*The **Microsoft Word Help Topics** dialog box appears,*
displaying help information on selected topic.

MICROSOFT ON THE WEB

Automatically connects you to Microsoft Internet sites, where
you can obtain online support, product information, and free
tools, such as Clip Art images and photos.

   Note: *You must have access to both the World*
   Wide Web and an Internet Browser to use
   this feature.

1. Click **Help**, **Microsoft on the Web** ... `Alt` + `H` , `W`

2. Select desired topic from submenu.

Your Internet browser will open with a Microsoft Internet site
address listed in the destination box.

WordPerfect Help

Provides help for WordPerfect users converting to Word. This feature allows you to use WordPerfect commands and navigation keys, and demonstrates how to perform tasks using Word commands.

> *Note: This option can also be selected with the General tab under Tools, Options. (See GENERAL OPTIONS, page 14.)*

1. Click **Help**, Word**P**erfect Help .... **Alt** + **H** , **P**

*The **Help for WordPerfect Users** dialog box displays.*

For information on specific WordPerfect commands:

   a. Click **Command keys** box .... **Alt** + **K** , **↑** **↓**
   and select desired command.

Information on the equivalent Word command displays in the right–hand section of the dialog box.

   b. Click [**Help Text**] .... **Alt** + **T**
   to display information as you use
   a specific WordPerfect command.

   OR

   Click [**Demo**] .... **Alt** + **D**
   to view a demo of WordPerfect command.

2. Click [**Options...**] .... **Alt** + **O**
   to choose WordPerfect navigation keys
   and other help options.

3. Select from the following Help options:

   • **Help for WordPerfect Users** .... **Alt** + **W**

   • **Navigation Keys for WordPerfect Users** ...... **Alt** + **N**

   • **Mouse Simulation** .... **Alt** + **M**

   • **Demo Guidance** .... **Alt** + **G**

continued...

24

*When **Help for WordPerfect Users** is turned on, the **WPH** message in the status bar is bold.*

4. Click **Demo speed** box.............. `Alt`+`S`, `↑` `↓`
   and select desired speed.

5. Click desired Help type:

   - [**Help Text**] .... `Alt`+`T`

   - [**Demo**] .... `Alt`+`D`

6. Click [**OK**] .... `↵`
   to close **Help Options** dialog box.

7. Click [Close] .... `Esc`
   to close **Help for WordPerfect Users** dialog box.

ABOUT MICROSOFT WORD

*Displays the **About Microsoft Word** dialog box, containing the name of the registered user and the serial number for the current copy of Word. Also displays the **Microsoft System Info** dialog box, containing information about your computer and the **Windows** environment.*

1. Click **Help**, **About Microsoft Word**... `Alt`+`H`, `A`

   To access Microsoft System Information dialog box:

   Click [**System Info...**] .... `Alt`+`S`

   To access technical support:

   Click [Tech Support...] .... `Alt`+`T`

2. Click [**OK**] .... `↵`

WHAT'S THIS?

Provides information on screen elements that you indicate.

1. Click **Help, What's This?** .... Alt + H , T

   OR

   Press **Shift+F1** .... Shift + F1

The mouse pointer changes to: ▶?

2. Click on screen item you want information on.

A help box appears, displaying information on selected item.

3. Press **Escape** to exit **What's This?** .... Esc

NAVIGATE

Navigate Using Go To Command

Moves to a specific page, section, or item in a document.

1. Double–click anywhere on left half of status bar.

   OR

   Click **Edit, Go To** .... Alt + E , G

   OR

   Press **Ctrl+G** .... Ctrl + G

*The **Go To** dialog box displays.*

2. Click ⌧ Go To ⌧ .... Alt + G

3. Click the **Go to what** box .... Alt + O , ↑ ↓
   and select type of document item
   to go to (i.e., page, field, bookmark,
   footnote, etc.).

continued...

26

4. Click the **Enter** box........ |Alt|+|E|, *text* or *number*
   and type the name, number, or
   other descriptor of item to go to.

   Notes: *The name of the **Enter** text box varies*
   *depending on the option selected in the **Go***
   *to what list box (e.g., **Enter Page Number**,*
   ***Enter Field Name**, etc.).*

   Pages, sections, lines, footnotes,
   endnotes, tables, graphics, equations, and
   headings are automatically numbered from
   the beginning of the document.
   Bookmarks, fields, and objects are
   identified by names; and comments are
   identified by reviewer initials.

5. Click | Go To | ....|Alt|+|T|

   OR

   Click | Next . | / | Previous | ..... |Alt|+|T|/|S|
   to go to next or previous occurrence
   of the selected document item.

   OR

   a. Type **+** or **−** and the number of items....*number*
      (of selected type) forward or backward
      to move from current position in document.

   b. Click | Go To | ....|Alt|+|T|

6. Click | Close | ....|Esc|
   to exit **Go To** dialog box.

Navigate Using Keyboard

To Move:	Press:
One character right	→
One character left	←
One word right	Ctrl + →
One word left	Ctrl + ←
One paragraph up	Ctrl + ↑
One paragraph down	Ctrl + ↓
One newspaper–style column right	Alt + ↓
One newspaper–style column left	Alt + ↑
Up one line	↑
Down one line	↓
Beginning of line	Home
End of line	End
To top of window	Ctrl + Alt + Page Up
To bottom of window	Ctrl + Alt + Page Down
Up one screen	Page Up
Down one screen	Page Down
Top of previous page	Ctrl + Page Up
Bottom of next page	Ctrl + Page Down
Beginning of document	Ctrl + Home
End of document	Ctrl + End
Previous revision	Shift + F5

OVERTYPE MODE

Replaces existing text to right of cursor as you type.

> *Note:*   *You can also type over existing text by selecting it and typing.*

Double–click **OVR** message OVR in status bar.

OR

Press **Insert**.. Insert

> *Notes:*   *The OVR button on the status bar is bold when the overtype mode is activated.*
>
>   *The Insert key can also be used for pasting information from the Clipboard. (See EDIT OPTIONS, page 111.)*

PASTE

Inserts information placed on the Clipboard into your document using the Cut or Copy commands. (See COPY, page 6, and CUT, page 7.)

1. Place information to be pasted elsewhere in the Clipboard using **Copy** or **Cut** commands.

2. Place cursor in document where information from the Clipboard is to be pasted.

3. Click **Paste** button 📋 in **Standard** toolbar.

   OR

   Click **Edit**, **Paste** .... Alt + E , P

   OR

   Press **Ctrl+V** .... Ctrl + V

PRINT

1. Click **File**, **Print** .... `Alt`+`F`,`P`

   OR

   Press **Ctrl+P**... `Ctrl`+`P`

*The **Print** dialog box displays.*

2. a. Click **Name** box .... `Alt`+`N`,`↑``↓`
      and select desired printer.

   Note: This changes the default printer.

   b. Click ⌐ Properties ⌐ .... `Alt`+`P`
      to access options for the selected printer
      (choices vary for different printers).

3. Select from the following **Page range**
   options (default is **All**):

   • **All** .... `Alt`+`A`

   • **Curre_nt Page** .... `Alt`+`E`

   • **Pa_ges**.. `Alt`+`G`
     Type page number or page range .... *page range*
     separated by commas (e.g., 1, 3, 5–12).

   • **S_election** .... `Alt`+`S`
     (available only if specific information has been
     selected in the document).

4. Click **Number of _copies** box..... `Alt`+`C`, *number*
   and type number of copies to
   print (default is **1**).

5. Click **Print _what** box .... `Alt`+`W`,`↑``↓`
   and select option.

continued...

30

PRINT (CONTINUED)

To sort multiple copies in correct page order:

Select the **Collate** check box .... `Alt`+`T`

6. Click **Print** box .... `Alt`+`R`,`↑``↓`
   and select portion of document to print.

   To print to a PRN file, rather than a printer:

   a. Select **Print to file** .... `Alt`+`L`

   b. Click [**OK**] .... `↵`

*The **Print to File** dialog box displays.*

   c. Select a drive and folder to store new file in.

   d. Type file name .... *filename*

   e. Click [**OK**] .... `↵`

7. Click [**Options...**] .... `Alt`+`O`
   for additional print options. *(See **Print Options**, page 31.)*

8. Click [**OK**] .... `↵`
   to close **Print** dialog box and begin printing.

Print Using Current Settings

Prints the entire active document using the current print settings.

Click **Print** button 🖨 in **Standard** toolbar.

Print Options

Customizes default print settings for Word files.

1. a. Click **File**, **Print** .... `Alt`+`F`,`P`

   *The **Print** dialog box displays.*

   b. Click [**Options...**] .... `Alt`+`O`

   OR

   a. Click **Tools**, **Options** .... `Alt`+`T`,`O`

   *The **Options** dialog box displays.*

   b. Click [Print]

2. Select from the following **Printing Options**:

   - **Draft output** ....`D`
     to print document with minimal formatting.

   - **Update fields** ....`U`
     to have Word update all fields before printing.

   - **Update links** ....`L`
     to have Word update all information linked
     to other files before printing.

   - **Allow A4/Letter paper resizing** ....`E`
     to have Word automatically resize documents
     formatted for A4 size paper to fit on 8.5''
     by 11'' paper, and vice versa, depending on
     standard paper size used by selected printer.

   - **Background printing** ....`B`
     to enable Word to print file in background,
     while you continue working. This uses
     more system memory and may slow
     printing process.

- **Print PostScript over text** .... N
  to print PostScript code on top of document
  instead of beneath it.

- **Reverse Print Order**.................................... R
  to print file in reverse order.

3. Select from the following **Include with Document** options:

   - **Document properties** .... M

   - **Field Codes**.. F

   - **Comments** C

   - **Hidden text** I

   - **Drawing objects** .... O

4. Click **Print Data Only for Forms** .... P
   if desired, to print data in a filled-in
   online form, but not the form itself.

5. Click **Default tray**.......................... T , ↑ ↓
   and select desired paper tray.

   Note: Choices vary depending on the type of printer.

6. Click [OK] .... ↵

REDO

Repeat the Most Recent Action

Click **Redo** button 🗘 in **Standard** toolbar.

OR

Click **Edit**, **Repeat** .... Alt + E , R

OR

Press **Control+Y**....................................... Ctrl + Y

Repeat Series of Recent Actions

a. Click drop–down arrow next to **Redo** button ↻▾

A list of the most recent actions displays.

b. Select series of actions to repeat.

SELECT INFORMATION

*(Also see **SELECT INFORMATION IN TABLES**, page 188.)*

Select Entire Document

Click **E**dit, Select A**l**l .... Alt + E , L

OR

Press **Control+A** .... Ctrl + A

Select Information Using Mouse

To Select:	Do This:
Any item	Press and hold left mouse button while dragging over desired information until highlighted.
A word	Double–click on word.
A graphic	Click graphic.
A line of text	Bring cursor to left of line until it changes to arrow. Click to select line.
Multiple lines of text	Bring cursor to left of document information until it changes to arrow. Press and hold left mouse button while dragging arrow to select document information.
A sentence	Press and hold **Ctrl**, click anywhere in sentence.
A paragraph	Double–click to left of paragraph, or triple–click anywhere in paragraph.

continued…

34

To Select:	Do This:
Multiple paragraphs	Click left mouse button to left of top paragraph and hold while dragging across paragraphs to select.
Entire document	Triple–click left mouse button.
Vertical block of text	Hold **Alt** and left mouse button at the same time and drag across information to select.

> *Note:*   *You can also select information by placing cursor at starting point, holding down **Shift**, and clicking at end of desired selection.*

Select Information Using the F8 Key

*You can extend the amount of information selected in a document by activating the **Extend Mode**. The **F8** key turns on this command. When **Extend Mode** is turned on, the **EXT** message in the status bar is bold.*

*You can also turn on **Extend Mode** by double–clicking the **EXT** message in the status bar.*

Action: **Press:**

Extend selection F8

Reduce selection size .... Shift + F8

Select entire document .... F8 six times

Select section .... F8 five times

Select paragraph .... F8 four times

Select sentence .... F8 three times

Select word .... F8 twice

Turn off Extend Mode .... Esc

Select Information Using Keyboard

To Select:	Press:
One character to the right	Shift + →
One character to the left	Shift + ←
Beginning of word	Shift + Ctrl + ←
End of word	Shift + Ctrl + →
Beginning of line	Shift + Home
End of line	Shift + End
One line up	Shift + ↑
One line down	Shift + ↓
Beginning of paragraph	Shift + Ctrl + ↑
End of paragraph	Shift + Ctrl + ↓
One screen up	Shift + Page Up
One screen down	Shift + Page Down
Beginning of document	Shift + Ctrl + Home
End of document	Shift + Ctrl + End
Entire document	Ctrl + A

SPIKE

*The **Spike** is an AutoText tool you can use to collect and store two or more items from different locations, which you can then insert as a group into a document. You can add items to the Spike at any time.*

Move Information to Spike

1. Select information you want to move to Spike.

2. Press **Ctrl+F3**..[Ctrl]+[F3]

3. Repeat steps 1 and 2 to move additional information to Spike.

    Notes: *Information moved to a spike is cut from the original location, not copied. To prevent this, copy the selection to the clipboard before moving it to the spike. Then, after spiking it, paste the information from the clipboard back into the original location.*

    *To view the contents of the Spike see **AUTOTEXT**, page 84.*

Insert Information from Spike

Pastes grouped information from Spike to insertion point.

1. Place cursor where you want to insert information from Spike.

2. Press **Shift+Ctrl+F3**.....................[Shift]+[Ctrl]+[F3]

    Note: *This function clears the contents of the Spike. To insert information without clearing the Spike, see **AUTOTEXT**, page 84.*

UNDO
Undo the Most Recent Action

Click **Undo** button ⤺ in **Standard** toolbar.

OR

Click **Edit**, **Undo**....................................[Alt]+[E], [U]

OR

Press **Control+Z**...[Ctrl]+[Z]

OR

Press **Alt+Backspace**..............................[Alt]+[Backspace]

Undo Series of Recent Actions

1. Click drop–down arrow next to **Undo** button ⟲▾

A list of the most recent actions displays.

2. Select actions to undo.

USER INFORMATION

Changes information about the primary user.

1. Click **Tools**, **Options** .... `Alt`+`T`,`O`

*The **Options** dialog box displays.*

2. Click ⎹ User Information ⎸

3. Click **Name** box .... `Alt`+`N`, *user name*
   and type user name. Word uses
   user name as the default author
   name in the **Properties** dialog box
   when creating new documents.
   (See PROPERTIES, page 59.)

4. Click **Initials** box .... `Alt`+`I`, *user initials*
   and type user initials. Word
   uses user initials by default
   for comment marks. *(See
   COMMENTS, page 227.)*

5. Click **Mailing Address** box .... `Alt`+`M`, *address*
   and type your address. Word uses
   this address by default when creating
   envelopes. *(See ENVELOPES AND
   LABELS, page 249.)*

6. Click ⎹ OK ⎸ .... `↵`

38

MANAGE FILES

CLOSE ALL FILES

1. Hold **Shift** and click **File** menu.

2. Click **Close All** .... `C`

    *Note: Select **Yes** or **No** to save and close each
    file, if they already have file names. If a file
    has not been named, the **Save As** dialog
    box appears. (See **SAVE FILE**, page 54,.)*

CLOSE FILE

Double–click document **Control** menu button `📄`

OR

Click **File**, **Close** .... `Alt`+`F`,`C`

OR

a. Click document **Control** menu button `📄` .... `Alt`+`-`

b. Click **Close** .... `C`

OR

Press **Ctrl+W** .... `Ctrl`+`W`

    *Note: Select **Yes or No** to save and close the file
    if it already has a file name. If the file has
    not been named, the **Save As** dialog box
    appears. (See **SAVE FILE**, page 54.)*

CREATE NEW FILE

    *Note: New templates can be created from
    existing documents and templates.
    (See **TEMPLATES**, page 63, for more
    information.)*

Create New File Based on Default Template

Click **New** button [icon] in **Standard** toolbar.

OR

Press **Ctrl+N**..[Ctrl] + [N]

*A new document is automatically created based
on the blank default template.*

Create New File Using Menu

1. Click **File**, **New** .... [Alt] + [F], [N]

*The **New** dialog box displays.*

2. Click tab containing template or form template
   you want to use to create new document.

3. Select desired display option for template list:

   - [icon] **Large Icons**

   - [icon] **List**

   - [icon] **Details**

4. Click on individual template.......... [↑] [↓] [←] [→]
   icons to see previews of their
   formatting in **Preview** box, if desired.

5. Click desired template to base new file on.

6. Select desired file type from option box
   under **Create New**:

   - **Document**.. [Alt] + [D]

   - **Template**.. [Alt] + [T]

7. Click [OK] .... [↵]
   to create the new file.

40

FIND FILE

Searches for file by file name, location, properties, last modification date, and/or specific text contained in file.

1. Click **File Open** button 📂 in **Standard** toolbar.

    OR

    Click **File, Open** .... `Ctrl`+`F`,`O`

    OR

    Press **Ctrl+O** .... `Ctrl`+`O`

*The **Open** dialog box displays.*

2. Click **File name** box............... `Alt`+`N`, *filename*
    and type name of file to find.

    > *Note:* *You can use wildcard characters (* ***** *and* **?** *)*
    > *if you're not sure of the full file name.*

3. Click **Files of type** box.............. `Alt`+`T`, `↓` `↑`
    and select type of file to find.

4. Click **Text or property** box .... `Alt`+`X`, *text*
    and type text or file property contained in
    file to find. Enclose phrases with quotation
    marks. *(See **PROPERTIES**, page 59.)*

5. Click **Last modified** .... `Alt`+`M`, `↓` `↑`
    and select time of last modification
    to file you want to find.

6. Click **Look in** box .... `Alt`+`I`, `↓` `↑`, `↵`
    and select drive to search.

*A list of folders and files appears in window
beneath **Look in** box.*

7. Double–click folder and subfolders to search.

continued.

8. Click [Find Now] .... Alt + F

*A list of found files displays in window below **Look in** box.*

9. Double–click file name from file window to open.

OR
To create a new search:

Click [New Search] .... Alt + W

Advanced File Find

1. Follow steps 1–7 under **Find File**, previous page.

2. Click [Advanced...] .... Alt + A

*The **Advanced Find** dialog box displays.*

3. Click **Look in** box .... Alt + I , ↓ ↑
   and select drive to search.

4. Click **Search subfolders**, if desired .... Alt + H

5. Select desired type of search:

   • Click **And** .... Alt + N
     to find only those files that meet all of
     your criteria.

   • Click **Or** .... Alt + R
     to find all files that match any of your criteria.

6. Click **Property** box .... Alt + P , ↓ ↑
   and select file property to search
   for: *(See **PROPERTIES**, page 59.)*

continued...

42

7. Click **Condition** box .... `Alt`+`C` , `↓` `↑`
    and select condition to find.

8. Click **Value** box.......................... `Alt`+`U` , *value*
    and type value to find.

9. Click [A̲dd to List   ] .... `Alt`+`A`

10. Repeat steps 6–9 to specify next set of criteria.

11. Click [F̲ind Now   ] .... `Alt`+`F`

    To create a new search:

    Click [Ne̲w Search   ] .... `Alt`+`W`

    To delete a search:

    Click [D̲elete   ] .... `Alt`+`D`

    To save a search:

    Click [S̲ave Search...   ] .... `Alt`+`S`

    To open a previously saved search:

    Click [O̲pen Search...   ] .... `Alt`+`O`

FORMS

*Creates an on–screen form to be filled in online, or a printed form to
be filled in by hand. All forms contain **form fields**, where users can
enter information. A printed form can contain two types of form
fields, **text** and **check box**, which users can fill in on paper.
Online forms can contain three types of form fields, **text**, **check
box**, and **drop–down list**, all of which appear on–screen for users
to type data into. You can also attach macros and customized Help
text to online forms to make them easier to fill out*

Create Forms

CREATE PRINTED FORM

1. Click **New document** button ⬚ in **Standard** toolbar.

   OR

   Press **Ctrl+N**...Ctrl + N

2. Open **Forms** toolbar. *(See **TOOLBARS**, page 82.)*

3. Design a form layout, as desired.

   *Note: You may want to insert or draw a table; add borders and shading; or add text boxes as placeholders for text blocks, graphics, or charts. (See **TABLES**, page 184; and **BORDERS AND SHADING**, page 90; and **TEXT BOXES**, page 178.)*

4. Add desired text and graphics. Include headings, questions to be answered, choices to be selected from etc. *(See **PICTURES AND OTHER OBJECTS**, page 159, and **FORMAT/EDIT**, page 84.)*

5. Insert text and/or check box form fields, as desired. *(See **Form Fields**, page 45.)*

6. Click **Protect Form** button 🔒 in **Forms** toolbar. *(See **PROTECT DOCUMENT**, page 231.)*

7. Save and print the form. *(See **SAVE FILE**, page 54, and **CLOSE FILE**, page 38.)*

CREATE ONLINE FORM

Save online forms as templates. That way, each user creates a copy of the form to fill out, without altering the "master" form.

1. Click **File**, **New** .... `Alt` + `F` , `N`

*The **New** dialog box displays.*

2. Click 🖹 **Blank Document**

3. Select **Template** under **Create new** .... `Alt` + `T`

4. Click `OK` .... `↵`

New template opens.

5. Display **Forms** toolbar. *(See TOOLBARS, page 82.)*

6. Design form layout as desired.

   Note: You may want to insert or draw a table; add borders and/or shading; or add text boxes as placeholders for text blocks, graphics, or charts. (See BORDERS AND SHADING, page 90; TABLES, page 184; and TEXT BOXES, page 178.)

7. Add desired text and graphics. Include headings, questions to be answered, choices to be selected from, etc. *(See PICTURES AND OTHER OBJECTS, page 159, and FORMAT/EDIT, page 84.)*

8. Insert form fields. *(See Form Fields, page 45.)*

9. Click **Protect Form** button 🔒 in **Forms** toolbar.

10. Save and close the template.

Form Fields
INSERT TEXT FORM FIELDS

Inserts a text form field where users can fill in information.

> Notes: *By default, form fields are shaded gray for easy online viewing. To turn off shading, click **Form Field Shading** button 🖼 on the **Forms** toolbar.*
>
> *A form field must be unprotected to be edited or designed. Click the **Protect Form** button 🔒 on the **Forms** toolbar to protect or unprotect a field.*

1. Create form. *(See **Create Forms**, page 43.)*
2. Display **Forms** toolbar. *(See **TOOLBARS**, page 82.)*
3. Place cursor in form where you want to insert text box field.
4. Click **Text Form Field** button on abl **Forms** toolbar.

A text form field box displays.

5. Double–click gray text form field box in document.

*The **Text Form Field Options** dialog box displays.*

6. Click **Maximum Length** box ..... Alt + M , *number* and type maximum number of characters or numbers for field entry.
7. Click **Type** box.................................... Alt + P and select a field type (Regular text, Number, Date, Current date, Current Time, or Calculation).

continued...

46

INSERT TEXT FORM FIELDS (CONTINUED)

8. Click **Bookmark** box beneath **Field**..... [Alt] + [B], *text*
   and type new name for field, if desired.

   Note: *By default, Word names all fields by type
   and number, (e.g., Text 3, Check Box 8,
   etc.) Changing a field name can make it
   easier to find.*

– For Online Forms –

9. Click **Default text** box .... [Alt] + [E], *text*
   and type text to appear as default
   entry, if desired.

   Note: *This option is not available if either **Current
   Date** or **Current Time** was selected in step 5.*

10. Click **Text Format** box............... [Alt] + [F], [↓] [↑]
    and select desired format for text in field.

11. Select from the following **Run Macro On**
    options, if desired:

    - Click the **Entry** box .... [Alt] + [Y], [↑] [↓]
      and select a macro to run automatically
      when the cursor enters the form field.

    - Click **Exit** box .... [Alt] + [X], [↑] [↓]
      and select a macro to run automatically
      when the cursor exits the form field.

12. Select **Fill–in Enabled** option .... [Alt] + [E]
    beneath **Field**, if desired, to enable online
    users to type information in field. Deselect
    this option to make the text field read–only.

13. Click [OK] .... [↵]

INSERT CHECK BOX FIELD

1. Create form. *(See **Create Forms**, page 43.)*

2. Display **Forms** toolbar. *(See **TOOLBARS**, page 82.)*

3. Place cursor in form where you want check box.

4. Click **Check Box Form Field** button ☑
   on **Forms** toolbar.

A check box appears at insertion point.

5. Double–click gray check box field.

*The **Check Box Form Fields Options** dialog box displays.*

6. Select desired **Check Box Size**:

   - Click **Auto** .... `Alt`+`A`
     to make check box the same point size as
     surrounding text in field.

   - Click **Exactly** .... `Alt`+`E`, *number*
     and type a point size for check box.

7. Click **Bookmark** box beneath **Field** .... `Alt`+`B`, *text*
   and type new name for field, if desired.

   *Note: By default, Word names all fields by type and
            number, (e.g., Text 3, Check Box 8) Changing
            a field name can make it easier to find.*

– For Online Forms –

8. Select desired **Default Value**:

   - Click **Not Checked** .... `Alt`+`K`
     to leave box empty by default.

   - Click **Checked** .... `Alt`+`D`
     to have box checked by default. (Online
     users then have to press the spacebar to
     deselect the check box.)

continued...

48

INSERT CHECK BOX FIELD (CONTINUED)

9. Select from the following **Run Macro On** options, if desired:

   - Click the **Entry** box .... `Alt`+`Y`, `↑` `↓`
     and select a macro to run automatically
     when the cursor enters the form field.

   - Click **Exit** box...................... `Alt`+`X`, `↑` `↓`
     and select a macro to run automatically
     when the cursor exits the form field.

10. Select **Check box enabled** option .... `Alt`+`N`
    beneath **Field** if desired, to enable online
    users to type information in field. Deselect
    this option to make the check box read-only.

11. Click `OK` .... `↵`

INSERT DROP–DOWN FORM FIELD IN ONLINE FORM

> *Note: This option is only available for online forms.*

1. Create online form. *(See CREATE ONLINE FORM, page 44.)*

2. Display **Forms** toolbar. *(See TOOLBARS, page 82.)*

3. Place cursor in document where you want
   to insert drop–down form field.

4. Click **Drop–Down Form Field** button 📑 on
   Forms toolbar.

A drop–down field appears at the insertion point.

5. Double–click the drop–down field.

*The **Drop–Down Form Field Options** dialog box displays.*

6. Click **Drop-Down Item** box............. `Alt`+`D`, *text*
   and type item to include in drop–down list.

continued.

49

INSERT DROP–DOWN FORM FIELD IN ONLINE FORM (CONT)

7. Click [**Add ▸▸**] .... `Alt`+`A`

8. Repeat steps 6–7 until finished adding items to list.

   To remove an item from the drop–down list:

   a. Click **Items in Drop–** .... `Alt`+`I`, `↑``↓`
   Down List box and select
   item to remove.

   b. Click [**Remove**] .... `Alt`+`R`

   To reorder items in drop–down list:

   a. **Click Items in Drop–** .... `Alt`+`I`, `↑``↓`
   Down List box and select
   item to move.

   b. Click **Move Up** or **Move Down** button..... `↑`/`↓`

9. Select from the following **Run Macro On**
   options, if desired:

   • Click the **Entry** box .... `Alt`+`Y`, `↑``↓`
   and select a macro to run automatically
   when the cursor enters the form field.

   • Click **Exit** box .... `Alt`+`X`, `↑``↓`
   and select a macro to run automatically
   when the cursor exits the form field.

10. Click **Bookmark** box beneath **Field** .... `Alt`+`B`, *text*
    and type new name for field, if desired.

    Note: *By default, Word names all fields by type and*
    number, (e.g., Text 3, Check Box 8) Changing
    a field name can make it easier to find.

50

11. Select **Drop–Down Enabled** option........ Alt + N
    beneath **Field**, if desired, to enable online
    users to select or type information in field. Deselect
    this option to make drop–down list read–only.

12. Click [OK] .... ↵

INSERT FORM FIELD HELP IN ONLINE FORM

*Adds custom Help messages to online form field, which display to
help users when cursor is in field. (Also see **HELP**, page 16.)*

> Note: *This option is only available for online
>   forms, and will not work with printed forms.*

1. Double–click an existing form field.

*The **Options** dialog box for the selected form field displays.*

2. Click [**Add Help Text...**] .... Alt + T

*The **Form Field Help Text** dialog box displays.*

**To add a help message to display automatically
in status bar when cursor enters field:**

a. Click [Status Bar] .... Alt + S

b. Select one of the following **Status Bar** options:

   • Click **None** .... Alt + N
     to omit help message.

   • Click **AutoText Entry** .... Alt + A , ↑ ↓
     and select desired AutoText entry
     to be displayed as Help text.

   • Click **Type Your Own**............... Alt + T , *text*
     and type custom Help text to display.

continued.

INSERT FORM FIELD HELP IN ONLINE FORM (CONTINUED)

To add a help message to display when cursor is in field and user presses F1:

a. Click `Help Key (F1)` .... `Alt`+`K`

b. Select one of the following **Help key** options:

- Click **None** .... `Alt`+`N`
  to omit help message.

- Click **AutoText Entry** .... `Alt`+`A`, `↑` `↓`
  and select desired AutoText entry
  to display as Help text.

- Click **Type Your Own** .... `Alt`+`T`, *text*
  and type custom Help text to display.

3. Click `OK` .... `↵`

Fill in Online Form

1. Click **File**, **New** .... `Alt`+`F`, `N`

*The **New** dialog box opens.*

2. Click icon for desired form template.

3. Click **Document** under **Create New** .... `Alt`+`D`

4. Click `OK` .... `↵`

5. Fill in form.

   To navigate through form:

   Click a form field or use following keystroke methods:

   - Move to next field .... `Tab`

   - Move to previous field .... `Shift`+`Tab`

continued...

52

FILL IN ONLINE FORM (CONTINUED)

- Display items .... `F4` or `Alt`+`↓`
  in drop–down form field.

- Move to item in open drop–down list .... `↑` `↓`

- Click or clear check box .... `Space` or `X`

- Insert tab in text form field .... `Ctrl`+`Tab`

6. Click **File**, **Save As** .... `Alt`+`F`, `A`

*The **Save As** dialog box opens.*

7. Print, save, or close new form document.
   *(See **SAVE FILE**, page 54; **CLOSE FILE**,
   page 38; and **PRINT**, page 29.)*

OPEN FILE

*Opens existing Word documents and templates, and allows you
to import files from other applications.*

> Note: In addition to the **File**, **Open** command,
> you can also open a recently used file from
> the file list that appears at the bottom of
> the **File** menu. Under **Tools**, **Options** click
> the **General** tab to change the number of
> recently used files that appear in the list.
> *(See **GENERAL OPTIONS**, page 14, for
> more information.)*

1. Click **File Open** button 📂 in **Standard** toolbar.
   OR
   Click **File**, **Open** .... `Alt`+`F`, `O`
   OR
   Press **Ctrl+O** .... `Ctrl`+`O`

*The **Open** dialog box displays.*

continued.

2. Click desired display option for file list:

   - 📋 **List**
   - 🗒️ **Details**
   - 🗒️ **Properties**
   - 🗒️ **Preview**

3. Click **Look in** box............... Alt + ↓ , ↑ ↓ , ↵
   and select drive containing file to open.

A list of folders and files appears in window beneath
Look in *box.*

4. Double–click the directory folder
   and subfolders containing desired file.

   To move to previous folder level:

   Click **Up One Level** icon 🔼

   To open Favorites folder:

   Click **Favorites** icon 📁

   To add current folder to Favorites folder:

   Click **Add to Favorites** icon 📁

   To search folders on the Internet:

   Click **Search the Web** icon 🔍

   To access additional commands and settings:

   Click **Commands and Settings** icon 📄

5. Select file to open .... ↑ ↓

6. Click ⬚ OK ⬚ .... ↵

54

SAVE FILE

Saves without exiting file.

1. Click **Save** button 🖫 in **Standard** toolbar.

   OR

   Click **File**, **Save** .... `Alt`+`F`, `S`

   OR

   Press **Ctrl+S** .... `Ctrl`+`S`

   Note: *If you are saving a new, unnamed file,*
   proceed to step 2.

*The **Save As** dialog box displays.*

2. Click desired display option for file list:

   - 📇 **List**
   - 📇 **Details**
   - 📇 **Properties**

3. Click **Save in** box.............. `Alt`+`I`, `↓`, `↑`, `↵`

*A list of folders and files appears in window beneath **Save in** box.*

4. Double–click directory folder and subfolder
   to save in. (Default is **C:\ My Documents**.)

   To change to previous folder level:

   Click **Up One Level** icon 📁

   To open Favorites folder:

   Click **Favorites** icon 📁

   To create new folder:

   Click **Create New Folder** icon 📁

continued.

5. Click **File name** box .... Alt + N, *name*
   and type new file name.

6. Click **Save as type** box............ Alt + T, ↓ ↑
   and select type of file to save
   [default is **Word Document (*.doc)**].

   Note: *The available file types vary depending on choices made during program installation.*

   To access additional save options:

7. Click Options... .... Alt + P
   *(See **Save Options**, page 56, for more information.)*

   To access additional commands and settings:

   Click **Commands and Settings** icon

8. Click OK .... ↵

   Notes: *Depending on choices selected in **Save Options**, the **Properties** dialog box may be displayed. (See **PROPERTIES**, page 59, and **Save Options**, page 56.)*

Save File As

Saves file with a new name and/or different file format.

1. Click **File, Save As** .... Alt + F, A

   OR

   Press **F12**.. F12

2. Follow steps 2–8 under **SAVE FILE**, above.

Save Options

Customizes default save settings.

1. a. Click **Tools**, **Options** .... `Alt` + `T` , `O`

*The **Options** dialog box displays.*

    b. Click [Save   ]

2. Select from the following save options:

- **Always create backup copy** .... `Alt` + `B`

- **Allow fast saves** .... `Alt` + `F`
  to save only changes to the original document.

- **Prompt for document properties** .... `Alt` + `I`
  to have **Properties** dialog box automatically
  open the first time you save a document.

- **Prompt to save Normal template** .... `Alt` + `O`
  to have a message automatically
  displayed each time you quit Word,
  asking if you want to save any changes
  made to default template settings.

- **Embed TrueType fonts** .... `Alt` + `E`
  to store true type fonts used in file along
  with the file, so that others can read and
  print the file with the correct fonts, even if
  they don't have the selected fonts installed
  on their computer.

- **Save data only for forms** .... `Alt` + `D`
  to save data in filled-in online forms,
  but not the forms themselves.

- **Allow background saves** .... `Alt` + `A`
  to enable Word to save a file in the background,
  while you continue working in Word.

continued..

- **Save AutoRecovery info every**............. `Alt`+`S`
  to have Word automatically create an
  AutoRecover file at the interval you select.

  Type number in minutes .... *number*
  for AutoRecover interval (default is **10 minutes**).

3. Click **Save Word files as**.......... `Alt`+`W`, `↓` `↑`
   and select the file format in which
   to save files in by default.

4. Select **File Sharing Options** for current document:

   a. Click **Password to open**.... `Alt`+`P`, *password*
      box and type password to
      use to protect document from
      being opened by others.

   Note: *Users who do not know the right*
   reservation password can open a
   *document by selecting the **Read Only***
   *check box in the **File Open** dialog box.*

   b. Click **Password to modify** ... `Alt`+`Y`, *password*
      box and type password to
      use to prevent unauthorized
      users from making changes to
      a document.

   Note: *Use this option to allow others to view a*
   document, while allowing only authorized
   users to edit the document.

   c. Click **Read-Only Recommended** .... `Alt`+`R`
      check box to recommend, but not require,
      that users open a document as read–only.

5. Click `OK` .... `↵`

58

Change Default Storage Folder

*The default **Save in** folder for Word 97 documents is **My Documents**. You can change the default **Save in** folder in the File Locations tab under **Tools**, **Options**.*

1. Click **Tools**, **Options** .... `Alt`+`T`,`O`

   *The **Options** dialog box displays.*

2. Click [File Locations]

3. Click **File Types** list box............ `Alt`+`F`,`↑``↓`
   and select file type for which you
   want to change default storage location.

4. Click [**OK**] .... `↵`

   *The **Modify Location** dialog box displays.*

5. Click **Folder name** box .... `Alt`+`N`
   and type path to folder to set as new
   storage default.

   OR

   a. Click **Look in** box .... `Alt`+`I`,`↑``↓`
      and select drive containing folder
      to set as storage default.

   *A list of folders displays in window beneath **Look in** box.*

   b. Double–click folders and subfolders
      in list until path to desired storage
      folder displays in **Folder name** box.

   c. Click [**OK**] .... `↵`

continued.

To create a new folder:

a. Click **Create new folder** icon 🗀

*The **New Folder** dialog box displays.*

b. Click **Name** box .... **Alt** + **N**, *name*
   and type new folder name.

c. Click [OK] .... ⏎
   to close **Create new folder** dialog box.

6. Click [OK] .... ⏎
   to close **Options** dialog box.

PROPERTIES

File properties are details about a file that help differentiate it from other files. There are three types of properties: preset, custom, and automatic. Preset properties are categories of information that Word automatically lists for you to fill in (e.g., title, author, subject, etc.). Custom properties are categories of information that you create and fill in for specific files. Automatic properties are statistics that Word automatically catalogs for each document, such as page count and file size.

Display General Properties

Displays general file information, such as file type and location, which Word automatically catalogs for each file.

1. Click **File**, **Properties** .... **Alt** + **F**, **I**

*The **Properties** dialog box displays.*

2. Click [General]

3. Click [OK] .... ⏎

60

Store Summary Information

Stores summary information (title, author, subject, etc.) that you define for the current document, to make it easier to find.

1. Click **File**, **Properties** .... `Alt`+`F`,`I`

*The **Properties** dialog box displays.*

2. Click `Summary`

3. Click **Title** box .... `Alt`+`T`, *title*
   and type title.

4. Click **Subject** box .... `Alt`+`S`, *subject*
   and type subject.

5. Click **Author** box .... `Alt`+`A`, *author*
   and type author name.

6. Click **Company** box .... `Alt`+`O`, *company*
   and type company name.

7. Click **Category** box .... `Alt`+`E`, *category*
   and type category.

8. Click **Keywords** box .... `Alt`+`K`, *keywords*
   and type keywords.

9. Click **Comments** box .... `Alt`+`C`, *comments*
   and type comments.

10. Click `OK` .... `↵`

Display Document Statistics

Displays detailed statistics (e.g., last modification date, date created, etc.), which Word automatically calculates and lists for active document.

1. Click **File**, **Properties** .... `Alt`+`F`, `I`

*The **Properties** dialog box displays.*

2. Click `Statistics`

3. Click `OK` .... `↵`

Display Document Contents

Lists the different elements of active document, such as macros, headings, or embedded objects.

1. Click **File**, **Properties** .... `Alt`+`F`, `I`

*The **Properties** dialog box displays.*

2. Click `Contents`

3. Click `OK` .... `↵`

Store Custom Properties

Stores, and displays custom properties that you create and define for active document.

1. Click **File**, **Properties** .... `Alt`+`F`, `I`

*The **Properties** dialog box displays.*

2. Click `Custom`

3. Click the **Name** box .... `Alt`+`N`, *name*
   and type property name, (e.g., "Typist" for
   a property identifying who typed a document).

4. Click the **Type** box .... `Alt`+`T`, `↓` `↑`
   and select type of value for property to
   record (text, date, number, or yes/no value).

continued...

62

5. Click the **Value** box...................... `Alt`+`V`, *value*
    and type value to assign, (e.g., typist's name).

    *Note: The value typed in step 5 must match the
             type of property value entered in step 4. For
             example, if you selected a date in step 4, the
             value entered in step 5 must be a date.*

6. Select **Link to Content**, check box .... `Alt`+`L`
    if desired, to link the property to
    specific file contents, such as a bookmark,
    heading, or Excel worksheet cell.

    *Note: This option is only available if you have
             defined specific contents in the active
             document, such as macros or headings.*

7. Click the **Source** box................. `Alt`+`S`, `↓``↑`
    and select the file element (macro,
    bookmark, etc.) to link property to.

    *Note: Linking a property to a file element can
             make the file easier to find. (For example,
             you might create a custom property for all
             dictated files and link the property to the
             bookmark containing the typist's name in
             each file, so you can search for and
             identify all files typed by a specific person.)*

8. Click [Add] .... `Alt`+`A`

    *New property appears in **Properties** list box.*

    To modify a custom property:

    a. Click **Properties** list box ...... `Alt`+`P`, `↓``↑`
        and select property to modify.

    b. Make desired changes in appropriate fields.

    c. Click [Modify] .... `Alt`+`D`

continued,

To delete a custom property:

a. Click **P**roperties list box ...... `Alt`+`P`, `↓` `↑`
   and select property to delete.

b. Click | Delete | .... `Alt`+`D`

9. Click | OK | .... `↵`

TEMPLATES

A template stores default settings and formatting (e.g., page and section setup, styles, AutoText entries, macros, headings, headers and footers, shortcut keys, menu assignments, and graphics) for a document type. When you use a template to create a new file, all of its settings apply to the new document, but the "master" template file remains unchanged.

*All documents in Word are patterned on templates, including the default blank new document. For this, Word uses a special global template, **NORMAL.DOT.**, which contains command information that is available to all Word documents, including those based on other templates. Command information contained in other templates, with the exception of styles, can also be made available globally. (See **Load Global Templates and Add–ins**, page 67.)*

*Word provides preformatted templates for a number of different document types, including faxes, memos, web pages, and resumes. For most documents, there are three template styles to choose from: **professional**, **elegant**, and **contemporary**.*

*Word also contains special automated templates called **wizards**. Wizards walk you through the process of creating specific types of documents, such as memos, letters, mailing labels, and reports. After creating a document using a wizard, you can save, edit, and format it just as you would any other document.*

Create New Template Based on Document

Creates new template based on an existing document.

1. Click <u>F</u>ile, <u>O</u>pen .... `Alt`+`F`,`O`

2. Open document to base new template on.
   (See OPEN FILE, page 52.)

3. Click <u>F</u>ile, Save <u>A</u>s........................... `Alt`+`F`,`A`

4. Click **Save as type** .... `Alt`+`T`,`↓``↑`
   and select **Document Template**.

*The **Templates** folder appears in the **Save <u>i</u>n** box. All templates saved in this folder will appear in the **General templates** tab of the **New** dialog box, when you click <u>F</u>ile, <u>N</u>ew. If desired, select another subfolder to store template in.*

5. Click **File <u>n</u>ame** .... `Alt`+`N`, *name*
   and type new template name.

6. Click [<u>S</u>ave] .... `↵`

7. Add styles, macros, text, and graphics to new template, as desired. Delete unwanted information. *(See PICTURES & OTHER OBJECTS, page 159, and FORMAT/EDIT, page 84.)*

8. Save and close new template when finished. *(See SAVE FILE, page 54, and CLOSE FILE, page 38.)*

Create New Template Based on Existing Template

1. Click <u>F</u>ile, <u>N</u>ew .... `Alt`+`F`,`N`

2. Click <u>T</u>emplate under **Create New**........ `Alt`+`T`

3. Double–click desired template.

Selected template opens on screen.

4. Click <u>F</u>ile, Save <u>A</u>s........................... `Alt`+`F`,`A`

continued.

CREATE DOCUMENT BASED ON EXISTING TEMPLATE (CONT)

*The **Templates** folder appears in the **Save in** box. All templates saved in this folder will appear in the **General Templates** tab of the **New** dialog box, when you click **File, New**. If desired, select another subfolder to store template in.*

5. Click **File name** box .... Alt + N , *name* and type new template name.

6. Click [Save] .... ↵

7. Add styles, macros, text, and graphics to template, as desired. Delete unwanted information. *(See **PICTURES AND OTHER OBJECTS**, page 159; and **FORMAT/EDIT**, page 84.)*

8. Save and close template. *(See **SAVE FILE**, page 54, and **CLOSE FILE**, page 38.)*

Modify Existing Template

1. Click **File, Open** .... Ctrl + O
   OR
   Click **File Open** button 🖼 in **Standard** toolbar.

2. Click **Look in** box .... Alt + ↑ , ↓ ↑ , ↵ and select drive containing template to modify.

3. Double–click folder containing template to modify.

4. Click **Files of type** box .... Alt + T , ↓ ↑ and select **Document Templates**.

5. Double–click template to modify.

Selected template opens on screen.

6. Make desired changes to information and formatting contained in template.

7. Save and close file. *(See **SAVE FILE**, page 54, and **CLOSE FILE**, page 38.)*

66

Attach Document Template

*Replaces the active document's current template, changing the settings (styles, macros, AutoText, shortcut keys, and custom toolbars) that apply to any new text you create. You can apply the newly attached template settings to already existing text by clicking the **Automatically update document styles** command.*

1. Click **Tools, Templates and Add–Ins...** `Alt`+`T`,`I`

*The **Template and Add–ins** dialog box displays. The template currently attached to the active document is displayed in the **Document template** box.*

2. Click **Document template** box .... `Alt`+`T`, *text* and type name of template to attach.

   OR

   a. Click `Attach...` .... `Alt`+`A`

*The **Attach Template** dialog box displays, opened to the path containing Word's template folders.*

   b. Double–click folder and subfolders containing desired template from list beneath **Look in** box.

*A list of the templates contained in selected folder displays in window beneath the **Look in** box.*

   c. Select template to attach.................. `↑`|`↓`

   d. Click `OK` .... `↵`

   Note: *Attaching a new template does not alter the existing document contents.*

   To automatically update document styles with styles from attached template:

   Click **Automatically update** .... `Alt`+`U`
   document styles check box.

continued.

3. Click [OK] .... [↵]

> *Note:* *Graphics and text from newly attached template are not automatically available. You must copy and paste them from the new template into the active document, or create a new document based on new template.*

Load Global Templates and Add–ins

Makes selected templates/add–ins available to all documents during current Word session.

1. Click **Tools, Templates and Add–Ins**..... [Alt]+[T], [I]

*The **Template and Add–ins** dialog box displays.*

2. Click **Global Templates**............... [Alt]+[G], [↑][↓]
   and add–ins box and select templates
   and add–ins to load globally.

   To add other templates and add–ins to the Global Templates and Add–ins list box:

   a. Click [Add...] .... [Alt]+[D]

*The **Add Template** dialog box displays, opened to the path containing Word's template folders.*

   b. Double–click folder and subfolders
      containing desired template from list
      beneath **Look in** box.

*A list of the templates contained in selected folder displays in window beneath the **Look in** box.*

   c. Select template to add........................... [↑][↓]

   d. Click [OK] .... [↵]

continued...

68

LOAD GLOBAL TEMPLATES AND ADD–INS (CONTINUED)

A loaded template or add–in program is only available for the current Word session. To save the template or add–in program, store it in your startup folder.

To remove a template or add–in from the Global Templates and Add–ins list box:

a. Click template or add–in to remove....... ⬆️⬇️

b. Click ☐ **Remove** .... Alt + R

*The **Remove** button is not available if the template to be removed is located in your startup folder.*

c. Click ☐ **OK** .... ↵

Notes: *You can unload a template or add–in without removing it from the **Global Templates and Add–ins** box, by clearing the check box next to its name.*

Unloading a template stored in your startup folder only unloads it during current Word session. It will be automatically reloaded the next time you start Word.

Organizer

Displays, copies, deletes, and renames styles, AutoText, toolbars, and macros attached to documents or templates.

1. Click **Tools, Templates and Add–Ins**... Alt + T , I

*The **Template** and **Add–ins** dialog box displays.*

2. Click ☐ **Organizer...** .... Alt + O

continued...

*The **Organizer** dialog box displays, containing four tabs: **Styles**, **AutoText**, **Toolbars**, and **Macros Project Items**. The available commands in each of the tabs are identical.*

*The file list box on the left side of the dialog box defaults to the current document, while the file list box on the right side defaults to NORMAL.DOT. The names of the file list boxes switch between **To** and **In**, depending on which file list box has items selected.*

3. Click the tab containing the elements to modify:

- Styles .... Alt + S
- AutoText .... Alt + A
- Toolbars .... Alt + T
- Macro Project Items .... Alt + M

To display a different document or template:

a. Click **Styles available in** .... Alt + V
   box below file list box on left side of
   dialog box.

   OR

   Click **Styles available in** .... Alt + B
   box below file list box on right side
   of dialog box.

b. Select a document or template ...... ↑ ↓ , ⏎

continued..

70

To open different document or template:

a. Click `Close File` .... `Alt`+`F`

   for file list box on left side of dialog box.

   OR

   Click `Close File` .... `Alt`+`E`

   for file list box on right side of dialog box.

b. Click `Open File...` .... `Alt`+`F`

   for file list box on left side of dialog box.

   OR

   Click `Open File...` .... `Alt`+`E`

   for file list box on right side of dialog box.

c. Follow procedures under **OPEN FILE**, page 52, to open desired file.

To copy items between different documents and templates:

a. Select an item to copy from **In** or **To** box.

Note: *Select multiple consecutive items by holding down **Shift** and clicking each item. Select multiple, nonconsecutive items by holding down **Control** and clicking each item.*

b. Click `Copy ▸▸` .... `Alt`+`C`

   to copy item from the left–hand list box to the right.

   OR

   Click `◂◂ Copy` .... `Alt`+`C`

   to copy item from right–hand list box to the left.

continued..

Note: If a copied item from the source file has the same name as an item in the destination file, a prompt will display asking if you want to overwrite the existing style entry.

To delete items from a document or template:

a. Select an item to delete from **In** or **To** box.

b. Click [**Delete**] .... `Alt`+`D`

c. Click [**Yes**] .... `Alt`+`Y`
to delete single item.

OR

Click [**Yes to All**] .... `Alt`+`A`
to delete all selected items.

To rename items in a document or template:

a. Select an item to rename from **In** or **To** box.

b. Click [**Rename...**] .... `Alt`+`R`

*The **Rename** dialog box displays.*

c. Type new item name .... *new name*
in **New name** box.

d. Click [**OK**] .... `↵`

4. Click [**Close**] .... `Esc`

VIEW OPTIONS

*Word provides many different ways to display and work with documents. In addition to the following choices, various other display options can be selected from the **View** tab under **Tools, Options**. (See **SCREEN DISPLAY OPTIONS**, page 78.)*

FULL SCREEN VIEW

Hides all portions of the screen that are not part of the document, such as the menu, toolbars, ruler, and scroll bars.

Click **View, Full Screen**........................... `Alt`+`V`,`U`

To exit Full Screen View:

Click | Close Full Screen | .... `Alt`+`C`

OR

Press **Escape**.. `Esc`

MASTER DOCUMENT VIEW

*Organizes and maintains long documents by dividing them into subdocuments. Word automatically assigns a unique file name to subdocuments by using the first characters in the first heading in a subdocument. Subdocuments are enclosed in a box and identified by the **Subdocument** icon (▤).*

*You can use **Master Document View** to group several Word documents together into one master document. This allows you to work with several documents at one time without having to open them individually.*

Click **View, Master Document**............... `Alt`+`V`,`M`

To switch to Master Document View from Outline View:

Click **Master Document View** button ▤ in **Outline** toolbar.

continued.

MASTER DOCUMENT VIEW (CONTINUED)

*Both the **Outline** and **Master Document** toolbars display in Master Document View. The Master Document toolbar buttons and their associated commands are as follows:*

Create Subdocument button. Creates a subdocument for selected headings.

Remove Subdocument button. Removes selected subdocument from a master document.

Insert Subdocument button. Inserts an existing Word document into a master document as a subdocument.

Merge Subdocument button. Merges selected subdocuments into one subdocument.

Split Subdocument button. Splits a subdocument into two subdocuments at location of cursor.

Collapse Subdocument button. Collapses subdocuments in active main document.

Expand Subdocument button. Expands subdocuments in active main document

Lock Document button. Prevents a subdocument from being edited. Locked subdocuments are represented by a padlock symbol (🔒) below the Subdocument icon.

NONPRINTING CHARACTERS

*Toggles display of nonprinting characters such as paragraph marks, tabs, and hidden text. (See **SCREEN DISPLAY OPTIONS**, page 78, for information on displaying specific types of nonprinting characters.)*

Click **Show/Hide** button ¶ on **Standard** toolbar.

OR

Press **Shift+Ctrl+8** .... Shift + Ctrl + 8

74

NORMAL VIEW

Click **Normal View** button 🔳
in lower left–hand corner of screen.

OR

Click <u>V</u>iew, <u>N</u>ormal .... `Alt`+`V`,`N`

OR

Press **Ctrl+Alt+N** .... `Ctrl`+`Alt`+`N`

OUTLINE VIEW

Displays document as outline, organized by Word's nine
***heading styles**. (See **STYLES**, page 146.)*

Click **Outline View** button 🔳
in lower left–hand corner of screen.

OR

Click <u>V</u>iew, <u>O</u>utline .... `Alt`+`V`,`O`

OR

Press **Ctrl+Alt+O** .... `Ctrl`+`Alt`+`O`

*In **Outline View**, paragraphs that do not use heading styles
have a hollow square symbol (▫) next to them. These
paragraphs are also referred to as **body text**.*

Format in Outline View Using Toolbar

*Once you are in **Outline View**, the **Outline** toolbar displays.
Outline toolbar buttons and commands are as follows:*

⬅️   ***Promote** button. Promotes selected paragraphs to the
previous heading style.*

➡️   ***Demote** button. Demotes selected paragraphs to the
next lower heading style.*

⏩   ***Demote to Body Text** button. Demotes selected
headings to Normal style body text.*

continued.

FORMAT IN OUTLINE VIEW USING TOOLBAR (CONTINUED)

Move Up button. Moves selected paragraphs above the preceding paragraph.

Move Down button. Moves selected paragraphs below following paragraph.

Expand button. Displays all text under selected paragraphs using heading styles.

Collapse button. Hides all text beneath selected paragraphs using heading styles.

Show Heading Level 1 button. Displays all paragraphs using heading 1 style.

Show Heading Level 2 button. Displays all paragraphs using heading styles 1–2.

Show Heading Level 3 button. Displays all paragraphs using heading styles 1–3.

Show Heading Level 4 button. Displays all paragraphs using heading styles 1–4.

Show Heading Level 5 button. Displays all paragraphs using heading styles 1–5.

Show Heading Level 6 button. Displays all paragraphs using heading styles 1–6.

Show Heading Level 7 button. Displays all paragraphs using heading styles 1–7.

Show All Heading Levels button. Switches between showing heading styles only or all heading styles and all body text.

Show First Line Only button. Displays first line only of body text paragraphs.

Show Formatting button. Displays text formatting.

Master Document View button. Displays **Master Document View**.

Format in Outline View Using Keyboard

*Formats information in **Outline View** using shortcut keys. Select the paragraphs or headings you want to format and use any of the following keystrokes:*

Formatting: Press:

Promote paragraph .... Shift + Alt + ←

Demote paragraph............................. Shift + Alt + →

Demote to body text........................... Shift + Ctrl + N

Move up .... Shift + Alt + ↑

Move down .... Shift + Alt + ↓

Expand text under heading................ Shift + Alt + +

Collapse text under heading .... Shift + Alt + -

Show all text or headings .... Shift + Alt + A

Display all text................................... ▪ * (keypad)

Display character formatting .... / (keypad)

Show first line or all body text........... Shift + Alt + L

Show all headings with .... Shift + Alt + #
specific heading style (type style number)

PAGE LAYOUT VIEW

Displays documents in their actual size, formatting, and layout.

Click **Page Layout View** button 🔲
in lower left–hand corner of screen.

OR

Click **V**iew, **P**age Layout .... Alt + V , P

OR

Press **Ctrl+Alt+P** .... Ctrl + Alt + P

PRINT PREVIEW

Click **Print Preview** button ▣ on **Standard** toolbar.
OR
Click **File, Print Preview**.......... .... Alt + F , V
OR
Press **Ctrl+Alt+I** .... Ctrl + Alt + I

*After switching to **Print Preview**, the **Print Preview** toolbar displays, containing the following commands:*

Print button. Sends the entire active document to print. (See **PRINT**, page 29.)

Magnifier button. Changes cursor to: 🔍

Click item to zoom on. Click **Magnifier** button again to return to editing mode.

One Page button. Displays one page at a time.

Multiple Pages button. Displays multiple pages simultaneously. (See **ZOOM**, page 82.)

Zoom Control box. (See **ZOOM**, page 82.)

View Ruler button. Toggles display of horizontal and vertical rulers.

Shrink to Fit button. Reduces document by one page by forcing small amounts of text to fit onto previous page.

Full Screen button. Hides all portions of the screen that are not part of the document. (See **FULL SCREEN VIEW**, page 72.)

Close button. Exits **Print Preview** and returns to previous document view.

Help button. Accesses Help for selected screen element. (See **HELP**, page 16.)

RULERS

Toggles display of horizontal and vertical rulers.

> *Note:* *Vertical rulers appear only in **Page Layout View** or **Print Preview**.*

Click **V**iew, **R**uler .... Alt + V , R

SCREEN DISPLAY OPTIONS

Customizes how Word displays your document on the screen.

1. Click **T**ools, **O**ptions .... Alt + T , O

2. Click ⊏ View ⊐

3. Select desired display options:

> *Note:* *Options vary depending on current page view (i.e., Normal view vs. Online Layout view, etc.). (See **VIEW OPTIONS**, page 72.)*

— In Normal or Outline View —

Select:	To:
Draft font	Hide character formatting and graphics, to speed up editing.
Picture placeholders	Display an empty box in place of each graphic in file to speed up time it takes to scroll through document.
A**n**imated text	Display animated text on screen. Deselect to view document as it will look when printed.
Scr**e**en Tips	Display comments when you place pointer on comment marks.
Highlight	Display text highlighting.
Boo**k**marks	Display brackets to indicate locations of bookmarks in document.

continued.

SCREEN DISPLAY OPTIONS IN NORMAL OR OUTLINE VIEW (CONT)

Select:	To:
Field codes	Display field codes instead of field results.
Field Shading	Shade field results (never, always, or when selected) for easy viewing (shading does not appear in printed document).
Tab characters	Display tab locations with horizontal arrows.
Spaces	Display spaces with dots.
Paragraph marks	Display paragraph endings with a ¶
Optional hyphens	Display optional hyphens with a ¬
Hidden text	Display hidden text.
All	Display all nonprinting characters.
Status bar	Display status bar.
Style area width	Set width for style area (the style area displays applied styles to the left of text). Type width in scroll box. (Type zero to hide style area.)
Horizontal scroll bar	Display horizontal scroll bar.
Vertical scroll bar	Display vertical scroll bar.
Wrap to window	Wrap text to window boundaries, rather than margin boundaries, for easier on-screen viewing (does not affect printing).

continued...

SCREEN DISPLAY OPTIONS (CONTINUED)

— *In Page Layout or Online Layout View* —

Select:	To:
Drawings	Display drawings. Deselect to speed up editing. (This option does not affect printed document.)
Object anchors	Display object anchors.
Text boundaries	Display dotted lines around page margins, columns, and objects.
Picture placeholders	Display an empty box in place of each graphic in file to speed up time it takes to scroll through document.
Animated text	Display animated text on screen. Deselect to view document as it will look when printed.
Screen Tips	Display comments when you place mouse pointer on top of comment marks.
Highlight	Display text highlighting.
Bookmarks	Display brackets to indicate locations of bookmarks in document.
Field codes	Display field codes instead of field results.
Field Shading	Shade field results (never, always, or when selected) for easy viewing (shading does not appear in printed document).

continued..

81

Select:	To:
Tab characters	Display tab locations with horizontal arrows.
Spaces	Display spaces with dots.
Paragraph marks	Display paragraph endings with a ¶
Optional hyphens	Display optional hyphens with a ¬
Hidden text	Display hidden text.
All	Display all nonprinting characters.
Status bar	Display status bar.
Vertical ruler (available only in Page Layout view.)	Display vertical ruler.
Enlarge fonts less than (available only in Online Layout view.)	Enlarge on–screen display of any characters smaller than the point size that you type in the scroll box.
Horizontal scroll bar	Display horizontal scroll bar.
Vertical scroll bar	Display vertical scroll bar.
Wrap to window	Wrap text to window boundaries, rather than to margin boundaries, for easier on–screen viewing (does not affect printing).

TOOLBARS

Displays toolbars and toolbar options.

> *Note:*   *See your Word documentation or online **Help** for information on customizing toolbars.*

1. Click **V**iew, **T**oolbars...................... `Alt` + `V` , `T`

*The **Toolbars** submenu displays. Toolbars that are checked are currently visible.*

2. Select toolbar to display .... `↑` `↓` , `↵`

> *Notes:*   *You can also access the Toolbars submenu by pointing at a displayed toolbar and clicking the right mouse button.*
>
> *Different toolbars appear on the submenu, depending on your activity.*

ZOOM

Set Zoom Using Menu

1. Click **V**iew, **Z**oom........................... `Alt` + `V` , `Z`

*The **Zoom** dialog box displays.*

2. a. Select one of the following **Zoom To** options:

   - **2**00%.. `Alt` + `2`
   - **1**00%.. `Alt` + `1`
   - **7**5%.. `Alt` + `7`
   - **P**age Width....................................... `Alt` + `P`
   - **W**hole Page....................................... `Alt` + `W`
   - **M**any Pages....................................... `Alt` + `M`

continued..

b. Click **Monitor** icon

c. Hold left mouse button and drag to select number of pages.

Note: *One Page and Many Pages options are only available if the document is in Page Layout View or Print Preview.*

OR

To select custom magnification setting:

Click **P̲ercent** box ....**Alt**+**E**, *number* and type a magnification percentage.

Set Zoom Using Mouse

1. Click drop–down arrow `100%` ↓ next to **Zoom Control** box in **Standard** toolbar.

2. Select a magnification setting.............↓ ↑ , ↵

   Note: *Whole Page and Two Pages options are only available in Print Preview.*

   OR

   a. Type number ....*number* for custom magnification setting in **Zoom Control** box.

   b. Press **Enter**...↵

FORMAT/EDIT
AUTOTEXT

*Stores text and graphics that you use frequently, so you don't have to recreate them each time. Examples of **AutoText** entries are company names, addresses, logos, and other information that you use frequently.*

*The names and contents of **AutoText** entries for the template attached to the current document can be printed. (See **PRINT**, page 29.) **AutoText** entries can also be renamed and copied to other documents and templates using the **Organizer**. (See **Organizer**, page 68.)*

Create AutoText Entry

1. Select information you want to store as **AutoText**.

    *Note: To store paragraph formatting in the
    AutoText entry, include a paragraph mark
    with the selected information.*

2. Click **I**nsert, **A**utoText .... `Alt`+`I`,`A`

    *The **AutoText** submenu displays.*

3. Click **AutoTe**xt .... `X`

    *The **AutoCorrect** dialog box opens to the **AutoText** tab.*

4. Click **Enter A**utoText .... `Alt`+`U`, *name*
    entries here box and type a name
    for the new AutoText entry.

5. Click **L**ook in box .... `Alt`+`L`, `↑`,`↓`, `↵`
    and select template to store
    AutoText entry in.

6. Click [**A**dd] .... `↵`

7. Click [OK] .... `↵`

Insert AutoText Entry

INSERT AUTOTEXT ENTRY USING MENU

1. Place cursor where you want to insert AutoText entry.

2. Click **Insert** .... Alt + I

3. Hold down Shift and click **AutoText** ...... Shift + A

The available AutoText entries and styles submenu displays.

4. Select the style linked to the .... ↑ ↓ , ↵
   desired AutoText entry.

A submenu displays listing AutoText entry names for the selected style.

5. Select desired **AutoText** entry .... ↑ ↓ , ↵

The AutoText entry is inserted into document.

INSERT AUTOTEXT ENTRY USING KEYBOARD

> *Note: Automatically inserts AutoText entries as formatted text.*

1. Place cursor in document where you want to insert an **AutoText** entry.

2. Type name .... *name*
   of an existing **AutoText** entry (or the first few letters that uniquely identify an entry).

3. Press **F3** F3

   OR

   Press **Ctrl+Alt+V** .... Ctrl + Alt + V

Edit AutoText Entry

1. Insert **AutoText** entry. (*See* **Insert AutoText Entry**, *page 85.*)

2. Edit entry as desired.

3. When finished editing, select edited entry.

   Note: *To store paragraph formatting in the AutoText entry, include a paragraph mark ¶ in the selected information.*

4. Click **Insert, AutoText** .... `Alt` + `I` , `A`

*The **AutoText** drop–down menu displays.*

5. Click **New** .... `N`

*The **Create AutoText** dialog box displays.*

6. Type original name .... *name* of **AutoText** entry.

Prompt displays asking if you want to redefine original entry.

7. Click **Yes** .... `↵`

Delete AutoText Entry

1. Click **Insert, AutoText** .... `Alt` + `I` , `A`

*The **AutoText** submenu displays.*

2. Click **AutoText** .... `X`

*The **AutoCorrect** dialog box opens, displaying the **AutoText** tab.*

3. Click **Enter AutoText entries here** .. `Alt` + `U` , `↑` `↓` box and select **AutoText** entry to delete.

4. Click **Delete** .... `Alt` + `D`

5. Click **OK** .... `↵`

BACKGROUNDS
Add Background Color

Adds background color to online documents or web pages. Do not use for printed documents. Backgrounds display only in Online View.

1. Click **Format, Background**.............. Alt + O, K
2. Click desired background color on **Fill** color grid.

   Note: Document view switches to Online Layout, and background color displays.

3. Click OK .... ↵

Add Gradient to Background Color

1. Click **Format, Background**.............. Alt + O, K
2. Click **Fill Effects**... .... F

*The **Fill Effects** dialog box displays.*

3. Click Gradient
4. Select from the following **Colors** options:

*The **Sample** box displays gradient choices.*

- Click **One color** .... Alt + O
   a. Click **Color 1**..... 1, ↑, ↓, ←, →, ↵
      box and select a color
      from **Fill** drop-down color grid.
   b. Click **Dark** or **Light**.......... Alt + K, ←, →
      bar and select a gradation level.

- Click **Two colors**........................... Alt + T
   a. Click **Color 1** .... 1, ↑, ↓, ←, →, ↵
      box and select color from
      Fill drop-down color grid.

continued...

88

ADD GRADIENT TO BACKGROUND COLOR (CONTINUED)

    b. Click **Color 2**.... `2`,`↑``↓``←``→`,`⏎`
        box and select a color from
        Fill drop–down color grid.

- Click **Preset**...................................`Alt`+`R`

    Click **Preset colors** ....`E`,`↑``↓`,`⏎`
    and select desired **Preset color**.

5. Click desired **Shading Styles** option:

- **Horizontal**...`Z`

- **Vertical** ....`V`

- **Diagonal up**...`U`

- **Diagonal down**...`D`

- **From corner**..`F`

- **From center**...`M`

6. Click **Variants** ....`Alt`+`S`,`↑``↓``→``←`
    and select a shading style.

7. Click `  OK  ` ....`⏎`

Add Texture to Background

1. Follow steps 1–2 under **Add Gradient to Background Color**, page 87.

2. Click `Texture`

*The texture **Sample** box displays.*

3. Click in **Texture**...........`Alt`+`T`,`↑``↓``→``←`
    window and select a texture.

    OR

    a. Click `Other Texture...` ....`Alt`+`O`

continued..

89

ADD TEXTURE TO BACKGROUND (CONTINUED)

*The **Select Texture** dialog box displays.*

    b. Open file containing desired texture.
      *(See **OPEN FILE**, page 52.)*

4. Click `OK` .... ⏎

Add a Pattern to Background

1. Follow steps 1–2 under **Add Gradient to Background Color**, page 87.

2. Click `Pattern`

3. Click **Pattern** window .. `Alt`+`T`, `↑` `↓` `←` `→`
   and select desired pattern.

4. Click **Foreground** box .... `Alt`+`F`

5. Select a foreground color ...... `↑` `↓` `←` `→`, ⏎
   from drop–down color grid.

6. Click **Background** .... `Alt`+`B`

7. Select a background color ..... `↑` `↓` `←` `→`, ⏎
   from drop–down color grid.

8. Click `OK` .... ⏎

Add a Picture to Background

1. Follow steps 1–2 under **Add Gradient to Background Color**, page 87.

2. Click `Picture`

3. Click `Select Picture...` .... `Alt`+`L`

*The **Select Picture** dialog box displays.*

continued...

90

ADD A PICTURE TO BACKGROUND (CONTINUED)

4. Open file containing picture to insert.
   *(See **OPEN FILE**, page 52.)*

*The selected picture file displays in the **Picture** box.*

5. Click [OK] .... ⏎

BORDERS AND SHADING

In Word 97, you can add borders and shading to any text, not just paragraphs. Select from a variety of shading patterns, foreground and background colors, and over 150 border styles, which can be applied to paragraphs, tables, and text.

Add Borders

Adds border(s) to any or all sides of page, table, paragraph, or selected text.

1. Select desired information to place border around.

2. Click **F**ormat, **B**orders and Shading .... [Alt] + [O], [B]

*The **Borders and Shading** dialog box displays.*

3. Click [Borders] .... [B]
   OR
   Click [Page Border] .... [P]
   to add borders around each page of document.

4. Select one of the following border styles:

   - ▤ **N**one.................................. [Alt] + [N]

   - ▥ **Bo**x.................................... [Alt] + [X]

   - ▥ **Sha**dow............................ [Alt] + [A]

continued.

- ▤ 3–**D** .... **Alt** + **D**

OR

To add borders to individual sides, rather than around entire selection:

a. Click ▥ **Custom** .... **Alt** + **U**

b. In **Preview** box, click on buttons or on diagram to indicate where to place borders.

Borders display in selected locations on Preview diagram.

5. Click **Color** box .... **Alt** + **C**, **↑** **↓**, **↵** and select desired border color.

6. Click border **Style** list box .... **Alt** + **Y**, **↑** **↓** and select border style.

To specify position of border on page:

a. Click [Options...] ....**O**

*The **Borders and Shading Options** dialog box displays.*

b. Select desired location options.

c. Click [**OK**] ....**↵**

To specify position of border in document:

Click **Apply to** box .... **Alt** + **L**, **↑** **↓**, **↵** and select desired border placement.

7. Click [**OK**] ....**↵**

92

Add Automatic Borders

1. Select information to place border(s) around.

2. Click drop–down arrow on **Borders** button ⊞ ▾ in **Formatting** toolbar.

3. Double–click border(s) to add from drop–down menu.

Remove Borders

1. Click anywhere inside border to be removed.

2. Click F**o**rmat, **B**orders and Shading... `Alt`+`O`, `B`

*The **Borders and Shading** dialog box opens.*

3. In **Preview** box, click on buttons or on diagram to indicate which border(s) to remove.

Selected borders disappear from the Preview diagram.

OR

Click **N**one .... `Alt`+`N`
to remove all borders around selection.

4. Click `OK` .... `↵`

Add Shading

Adds shading and pattern colors to selected text/paragraph.

1. Select information to add shading to.

2. Click F**o**rmat, **B**orders and Shading... `Alt`+`O`, `B`

*The **Borders and Shading** dialog box displays.*

3. Click `Shading` .... `S`

> Note: The **Shading** tab is not available if a graphic was selected in step 1.

continued.

93

ADD SHADING (CONTINUED)

4. Click **Apply to** box .... `Alt`+`L`, `↑` `↓`, `↵`
and select where to add shading
(to selected text or entire paragraph).

5. Select a shading color from **Fill** grid.

6. Click pattern **Style** box ..... `Alt`+`Y`, `↑` `↓`, `↵`
and select a shading percentage.

7. Click pattern **Color** box..... `Alt`+`C`, `↑` `↓`, `↵`
and select a pattern color.

To remove all custom shading and formatting:

Click **None** .... `Alt`+`N`

8. Click `OK` .... `↵`

BULLETS AND NUMBERING
Format Bulleted List

Formats selected information as a bulleted list using the
***Format, Bullets and Numbering** command.*

1. Select information to format as bulleted list.

2. Click **Format, Bullets and Numbering** .... `Alt`+`O`, `N`

*The **Bullets and Numbering** dialog box displays.*

3. Click `Bulleted` .... `Alt`+`B`

4. Click desired bullet format.

To remove bullets from selected information:

Click `None`

5. Click `OK` .... `↵`

94

CUSTOMIZE BULLETED LIST FORMAT

1. Click **F**ormat, **B**ullets and **N**umbering..... `Alt`+`O`,`N`

*The **Bullets and Numbering** dialog box displays.*

2. Click [**Bu**lleted] .... `Alt`+`B`

3. Click bullet format to customize.

4. Click [Cus**t**omize...] .... `Alt`+`T`

*The **Customize Bulleted List** dialog box displays.*

5. Click **Bu**llet character.............. `Alt`+`U`,`←``→`
   box and select a bullet shape.

   To select a bullet character not in current list:

   a. Click [**B**ullet...] .... `Alt`+`B`

*The **Symbol** dialog box displays.*

   b. Click **F**ont box.................... `Alt`+`F`,`↑``↓`
      and select font containing
      character to use as a bullet.

   c. Double–click desired bullet character.

   *Note: Clicking once on a character magnifies
              it for easier viewing.*

   To change font for selected bullet format:

   a. Click [**F**ont...] .... `Alt`+`F`

*The **Font** dialog box displays.*

   b. Follow steps 4–9 in **Font**, page 101.

   c. Click [**OK**] .... `↵`

continued...

To modify/remove bullet indent:

Click **Indent at** box .... `Alt`+`A`, *number*
beneath **Bullet Position** and type
desired bullet position (type zero to
remove bullet indent altogether).

To modify/remove hanging indent:

Click **Indent at** box .... `Alt`+`I`, *number*
beneath **Text position** and type desired
hanging indent position (type zero to
remove hanging indent altogether).

6. Click `OK` .... `↵`
   to apply selected bullet format.

Format Numbered List

Formats selected information as a numbered list using the
Format, ***Bullets and Numbering*** *command.*

1. Select information to format as numbered list.

2. Click **Format, Bullets and Numbering** .... `Alt`+`O`,`N`

*The **Bullets and Numbering** dialog box displays.*

3. Click `Numbered` .... `Alt`+`N`

4. Click desired number format.

   To remove numbers from selected information:

   Click `None`

5. Click `OK` .... `↵`
   to apply selected number format.

CUSTOMIZE NUMBERED LIST FORMAT

1. Click F**o**rmat, Bullets and **N**umbering..... `Alt`+`O`,`N`

*The **Bullets and Numbering** dialog box displays.*

2. Click [**N**umbered] .... `Alt`+`N`

3. Click **Numbered** format to customize.

4. Click [Cus**t**omize...] .... `Alt`+`T`

*The **Customize Numbered List** dialog box displays.*

   To change font for selected number format:

   a. Click [**F**ont...] .... `Alt`+`F`

*The **Font** dialog box displays.*

   b. Follow steps 4–9 in **Font**, page 101.

   c. Click [OK] .... `↵`

5. Click **N**umber style box .... `Alt`+`N`, `↑` `↓`
   and select desired number style.

6. Click **S**tart at box .... `Alt`+`S`, *number*
   and type starting number.

   To modify/remove number indent:

   a. Click **Number position** box .... `↑` `↓`
      and select a number position.

   b. Click **A**ligned at box .... `Alt`+`A`, *number*
      and type indent position for numbers
      (type zero to remove number indent altogether).

   To modify/remove hanging indent:

   Click **I**ndent at box................. `Alt`+`I`, *number*
   beneath **Text position** and type
   desired indent position for text (type
   zero to remove hanging indent altogether).

7. Click [OK] .... `↵`

Format Multilevel List

Formats selected information as a multilevel list using the
Format**, **Bullets and Numbering command.

1. Select information to format as a multilevel list.

2. Click F<u>o</u>rmat, Bullets and <u>N</u>umbering .... `Alt`+`O`, `N`

*The **Bullets and Numbering** dialog box displays.*

3. Click `O`u`t`line Numbered .... `Alt`+`U`

   *Note: This option is unavailable if a single
   paragraph formatted with a heading level
   style was selected in step 1.*

4. Click desired multilevel format.

   **To remove multilevel list formatting
   from selected information:**

   Click | None |

   *Notes: This option is available only if selected
   information is formatted with bullets
   or numbers.*

   *The **None** option removes all bullet and
   numbering options selected from any of
   the available tabs in the **Bullets and
   Numbering** dialog box.*

5. Click | OK | .... `↵`
   to apply selected multilevel format.

98

CUSTOMIZE MULTILEVEL LIST FORMAT

1. Click F**ormat, Bullets and N**umbering ..... `Alt` + `O` , `N`

*The **Bullets and Numbering** dialog box displays.*

2. Select | Outline Numbered | .... `Alt` + `U`

3. Click outline format to modify.

4. Click | Customize... | .... `Alt` + `T`

*The **Customize Outline Numbered List** dialog box displays.*

5. Click Le**v**el list box .... `Alt` + `V` , `↑` `↓`
   and select level to change.

6. Click **Bullet or N**umber style .... `Alt` + `N` , `↑` `↓`
   box and select a **bullet/number** style.

7. Click **S**tart at box .... `Alt` + `S` , *number*
   and type starting number or letter.

8. Click **P**revious level number .... `Alt` + `P` , `↑` `↓`
   box and select number formatting
   from previous levels that you want to
   include with subordinate levels.

   *Note: This option is unavailable if level 1 was
   selected in step 6.*

   To change font for selected multilevel list format:

   a. Click | Font... | .... `Alt` + `F`

*The **Font** dialog box displays.*

   b. Follow steps 4–9 in **Font**, page 101.

   c. Click | OK | .... `↵`

continued..

CUSTOMIZE MULTILEVEL LIST FORMAT (CONTINUED)

To modify/remove number/letter indent:

a. Click drop–down list box beneath......... ⬆️ ⬇️
   Number position and select desired
   alignment (left, right, or center).

b. Click **Aligned at** box .... Alt + A , *number*
   and type desired indent position for
   numbers/letters (type zero to remove
   number/letter indent altogether).

To modify/remove hanging indent:

Click **Indent at** box .... Alt + I , *number*
beneath **Text position** and type
desired indent position for text (type
zero to remove hanging indent altogether).

For more custom style options:

a. Click [More ⬇️] .... Alt + M

b. Click **Link level to style**....... Alt + K , ⬆️ ⬇️
   box and select style to attach to
   selected outline level (Word will
   automatically assign a number in the
   selected outline level to any paragraph
   formatted in attached style).

c. Click **Follow number with** ... Alt + W , ⬆️ ⬇️
   box and select character to be
   automatically placed between
   the list number and the first
   word in the paragraph.
   (Default is **Tab** character.)

continued...

100

   d. Click **ListNum field list name** ..... `Alt`+`T` , *name* and type label for lists generated using the **LISTNUM** field (**LISTNUM** fields generate lists that can contain more than one outline numbering level on a single line. See your online help for more information.)

   e. Select **Restart numbering after** .... `Alt`+`R` **higher list level**, if desired, to restart numbering at each new section.

   f. Click **Legal style numbering** .... `Alt`+`G` if desired, to change current outline numbers to equivalent Arabic values (e.g., Article IV becomes Article 4).

9. Repeat steps 5–8 to change formatting for additional levels.

10. Click [**OK**] .... `⏎` to apply selected multilevel list format.

Format Bulleted/Numbered Lists Using Toolbar

*Adds and removes bullets or numbering from selected information using the **Formatting** toolbar.*

1. Select information to format as bulleted or numbered list.

2. Click **Bullets** button 📑 in **Formatting** toolbar.

   OR

   Click **Numbering** button 📑 in **Formatting** toolbar.

   Note: *The last settings used to format bullets or numbers are applied to selected information.*

Create Automatic Numbered and Bulleted Lists

1. In a blank paragraph, type the starting number (followed by a period), or a bullet, asterisk, hyphen, dash, or similar character.

2. Press **Tab** key or space bar.

3. Type desired information for first item in list.

4. Press **Enter**...⏎

5. Repeat steps 2–3 for each additional item.

CHARACTER FORMATTING

Font

1. Select text with font to change.

2. Click **Format, Font**............................ **Alt**+**O**, **F**

   OR

   Press **Ctrl+D**..**Ctrl**+**D**

   *The **Font** dialog box displays.*

3. Click ⟨ Font ⟩ ....**Alt**+**N**

4. Click **Font** list box...................**Alt**+**F**, **↑** **↓**
   and select desired font.

5. Click **Font style** list box............**Alt**+**Y**, **↑** **↓**
   and select desired font style.

   Note: Choices vary with selected font.

6. Click **Size** list box....................**Alt**+**S**, **↑** **↓**
   and select desired font point size.

7. Click **Underline** box..................**Alt**+**U**, **↑** **↓**
   and select desired underline style.

continued...

102

8. Click **C**olor box ....⊞`Alt`+`C`,`↑``↓`
   and select desired color.

9. Select check boxes for desired font effects from window beneath **Effects**.

   *Note: To set custom superscript and subscript positions, see step 7 under **Character Spacing**, page 104.*

To use selected options as default settings for the current document and all new documents based on current template:

a. Click `Default...` ....`Alt`+`D`

b. Click `Yes` ....`↵`
   when confirmation dialog box appears.

   *Note: The default setting changes in **Fonts** will also be applied to like options under the **Character Spacing** tab. (See **Character Spacing**, page 104.)).*

10. Click `OK` ....`↵`

MODIFY FONT USING TOOLBAR

To Format: **Click:**

Fonts............................ `Times New Roman` `↓`

Point Size... `12` `↓`

Bold... `B`

Italic.. `I`

Underline.. `U`

MODIFY FONT USING KEYBOARD
To Format: **Press:**

All capital letters .... `Shift` + `Ctrl` + `A`

Bold .... `Ctrl` + `B`

Create Symbol font .... `Shift` + `Ctrl` + `Q`

Display nonprinting characters .... `Shift` + `Ctrl` + `*`

Go to font box (**Formatting** toolbar) ...... `Shift` + `Ctrl` + `F`

Display hidden text .... `Shift` + `Ctrl` + `H`

Italicize .... `Ctrl` + `I`

Letters – switch case .... `Shift` + `F3`

Go to point size box (**Formatting** toolbar) .... `Shift` + `Ctrl` + `P`

Point size – decrease 1 point .... `Ctrl` + `[`

Point size – decrease .... `Shift` + `Ctrl` + `<`
to next available point size

Point size – increase 1 point .... `Ctrl` + `]`

Point size – increase to next .... `Shift` + `Ctrl` + `>`
available point size

Remove formatting .... `Shift` + `Ctrl` + `Z`

Small capital letters .... `Shift` + `Ctrl` + `K`

Subscript .... `Ctrl` + `=`

Superscript .... `Shift` + `Ctrl` + `=`

Underline – single .... `Ctrl` + `U`

Underline – double .... `Shift` + `Ctrl` + `D`

Underline – word only .... `Shift` + `Ctrl` + `W`

104

Character Spacing

1. Select text with formatting to change.

2. Click **Format, Font** .... `Alt` + `O`, `F`

   OR

   Press **Ctrl+D** .... `Ctrl` + `D`

   *The **Font** dialog box displays.*

3. Click `Character Spacing` .... `Alt` + `R`

4. Click **Scale** box .... `Alt` + `C`, *number*
   and type desired scale percentage.

5. Click **Spacing** box .... `Alt` + `S`, `↑` `↓`
   and select desired spacing option
   (**Normal, Expanded,** or **Condensed**).

6. Click **By** box .... `Alt` + `B`, *number*
   and type distance to place between characters.

7. Click **Position** box .... `Alt` + `P`, `↑` `↓`
   and select position in relation to
   baseline (**Normal, Raised,** or **Lowered**).

8. Click **By** box .... `Alt` + `Y`, *number*
   and type number of points to raise/
   lower text in relation to baseline, if necessary.

   *Note: This options is not available if
   Normal was selected in step 7.*

9. Click **Kerning for Fonts** check box .... `Alt` + `K`
   if desired, to have Word automatically
   adjust spacing between characters to
   make entire words look more evenly spaced.

   *Note: Kerning is only available for TrueType or
   Adobe Type Manager fonts.*

continued

10. Click **Po̲ints and above** box......![Alt]+![O], *number*
    and type desired point size.

    **To use selected options as default settings
    for current document and all new documents
    based on current template:**

    a. Click [**D̲efault...**] ....![Alt]+![D]

    b. Click [**Y̲es**] ....![Alt]+![Y]

       when confirmation dialog box appears.

    *Note: Selecting the **Default** button changes the
            defaults for options selected in both the
            Character Spacing tab and the **Fonts** tab.*

11. Click [**OK**] ....![↵]

Change Case

1. Select information with case formatting to change.

2. Click **Fo̲rmat, Change Cas̲e**............![Alt]+![O],![E]

   *The **Change Case** dialog box displays.*

3. Select one of the following case options:

   • **S̲entence case**.....................................![Alt]+![S]

   • **l̲owercase** ....![Alt]+![L]

   • **U̲PPERCASE** ....![Alt]+![U]

   • **T̲itle Case** ....![Alt]+![T]

   • **tO̲GGgle cASE**...................................![Alt]+![G]

4. Click [**OK**] ....![↵]

   *Note: You can also switch the case of selected text
           by pressing **Shift+F3**.*

Drop Cap

Formats selected text as a dropped capital letter.

1. Select letter or text you want to format as drop cap.

2. Click **Format**, **Drop Cap** .... `Alt` + `O`, `D`

*The **Drop Cap** dialog box displays.*

3. Select one of the following drop cap positions:

   - **None** .... `Alt` + `N`

   - **Dropped** .... `Alt` + `D`

   - **In Margin** .... `Alt` + `M`

4. Click **Font** box .... `Alt` + `F`, `↑` `↓`
   and select font to use for drop cap.

   > Note: This option is unavailable if **None** was
   >   selected in previous step.

5. Click **Lines to Drop** box .... `Alt` + `L`, *number*
   and type number of lines to
   extend drop cap downward.

   > Note: This option is unavailable if **None** was
   >   selected in step 3.

6. Click **Distance from text** box ... `Alt` + `X`, *number*
   and type amount of space to place
   between drop cap and body of paragraph.

7. Click `OK` .... `↵`

Insert Symbols/Special Characters

Symbols and *special characters* are characters that are not available on the keyboard, such as bullets, European letters, and trademark symbols.

SYMBOLS

Inserts characters from different character sets.

1. Place cursor where you want to insert symbol.
2. Click **I**nsert, **S**ymbol...................... Alt + I , S

*The **Symbols** dialog box displays.*

3. Click ⌷Symbols .... Alt + S
4. Click **F**ont box .... Alt + F , ↑ ↓
   and select font containing
   character to insert.
5. Double–click desired symbol character.

   *Note: Clicking once on a character magnifies it
           for easier viewing.*

   To assign selected character to a shortcut key:

   a. Click ⌷ **Shortcut Key...** .... Alt + K

*The **Customize Keyboard** dialog box displays.*

   b. Click C**o**mmands list box..... Alt + O , ↑ ↓
      and select symbol with key
      sequence to modify.

   c. Click **Press new shortcut key** ... Alt + N , *keys*
      box and type new key sequence.

   *Note: If the selected keyboard sequence is
           already assigned to another command, that
           command will be displayed in the **Press
           new shortcut key** box.*

continued...

108

SYMBOLS (CONTINUED)

    d. Click `Assign` .... `A`

       to assign new key sequence to symbol.

    Note: *Clicking **Assign** overwrites any pre-*
           existing command assignment for selected
           shortcut keys with current selection.

    e. Click `Close` .... `↵`

       to close **Customize keyboard** dialog box
       and return to the **Symbol** dialog box.

6. Click `Close` .... `↵`

SPECIAL CHARACTERS

1. Place cursor where you want to insert character.

2. Click **In**s**ert**, **Symbol** .... `Alt`+`I`, `S`

*The **Symbols** dialog box displays.*

3. Click `Special Characters` .... `Alt`+`S`

4. Click **Character** list box .... `Alt`+`C`, `↑` `↓`
   and select special character to insert.

To assign new shortcut key to selected character:

    a. Click `Shortcut Key...` .... `Alt`+`K`

*The **Customize** dialog box displays, opened to **Keyboard** tab.*

    b. Click **C**o**mmands** list box ..... `Alt`+`O`, `↑` `↓`
      and select character with key
      sequence to modify.

    b. Follow steps 5c–e in **Symbols**, above.

5. Click `Insert` .... `↵`

6. Click `Close` .... `↵`

SPECIAL CHARACTERS KEYBOARD SHORTCUTS

Special Character: Press:

Column break .... `Shift` + `Ctrl` + `↵`

Copyright symbol............................. `Alt` + `Ctrl` + `C`

Double closing Smart Quote .... `Ctrl` + `` ` ``

then `Shift` + `"`

Double opening Smart Quote..................... `Ctrl` + `` ` ``

then `Shift` + `"`

Ellipses .... `Alt` + `Ctrl` + `.`

Line break...................................... `Shift` + `↵`

Nonbreaking hyphen......................... `Shift` + `Ctrl` + `-`

Nonbreaking space .... `Shift` + `Ctrl` + `Space`

Optional hyphen................................ `Ctrl` + `-`

Page break..................................... `Ctrl` + `↵`

Registered trademark symbol............. `Ctrl` + `Alt` + `R`

Single closing Smart Quote .... `Ctrl` + `` ` ``, `'`

Single opening Smart Quote................. `Ctrl` + `` ` ``, `'`

Trademark symbol............................. `Ctrl` + `Alt` + `T`

Note: In addition to inserting **Smart Quotes** with
the above keystrokes, you can also set
AutoCorrect to automatically replace
straight quotes with **Smart Quotes**. (See
AUTOCORRECT, page 225, for more
information.)

110

Copy Character Formats

Copies and applies character formats to other text in document.

> Note: **Format Painter** *copies the applied character style and formatting of the first character of selected information. If a paragraph mark is selected, Word also copies the paragraph style, in addition to the character style. (See* **STYLES***, page 146, for more information.)*

COPY CHARACTER FORMATS USING FORMAT PAINTER

1. Select information containing character formatting you want to copy.

2. Click **Format Painter** button 🖌 in **Standard** toolbar to copy formatting of selected information to a single location.

   OR

   Double–click **Format Painter** button 🖌 to copy formatting to multiple locations.

The mouse pointer changes to: 🖌

3. Position pointer at starting point of information where copied character formatting will be applied.

4. Click and drag mouse to select information.

5. Release mouse button.

   If you double–clicked Format Painter button in step 2:

   a. Repeat steps 3–5 to copy character formatting to additional locations.

   b. Press **Escape** .... `Esc`
   to turn off **Format Painter**.

COPY CHARACTER FORMATS USING KEYBOARD

1. Select information with character formatting to copy.
2. Press **Shift+Ctrl+C** .... Shift + Ctrl + C
3. Select information to copy character formatting to.
4. Press **Shift+Ctrl+V** .... Shift + Ctrl + V

EDIT OPTIONS

Enables/disables various editing settings for default use in all Word files.

1. Click **Tools, Options** .... Alt + T , O

*The **Options** dialog box displays.*

3. Click [Edit]
4. Select from the following **Editing Options:**

- **Typing replaces selection** .... Alt + T
  to have Word automatically delete selected text when you start typing. Deselect this option to have Word insert newly typed text in front of selection without deleting it.

- **Drag–and–Drop text editing** .... Alt + D
  to enable drag–and–drop editing. *(See DRAG AND DROP, page 13.)*

- **When selecting, automatically** .... Alt + W
  select entire word to have Word automatically select an entire word when you select part of it.

- **Use INS key for paste** .... Alt + U
  to enable use of the **Insert** key to paste information from the Clipboard.

continued...

112

- **Overtype mode** .... `Alt`+`O`
  to have Word automatically replace existing
  text to the right of the cursor when you type.
  (See OVERTYPE MODE, page 28.)

- **Use Smart cut and paste** .... `Alt`+`S`
  to have Word automatically remove extra
  spaces and add needed spaces when you
  paste text from the Clipboard. *(See CUT,
  page 7, COPY, page 6, and PASTE, page 28.)*

- **Tab and backspace keys** .... `Alt`+`I`
  to set left indent to have Word automatically
  increase the left indent when you press the
  Tab key, and decrease it when you press the
  Backspace key.

- **Allow accented uppercase in French** ..... `Alt`+`A`
  to have Word automatically suggest accent
  marks for uppercase letters in text formatted
  in French. *(See LANGUAGE, page 230.)*

5. Click **Picture editor** box .... `Alt`+`P`,`↑``↓`
   and select application to use as
   the default picture editor.

   *Note: Choices vary depending on what
   applications you have installed.*

6. Click `    OK    ` .... `↵`

FIELDS

Fields *are placeholders for information that may change, such
as page numbers, dates, and time fields. You can also use
fields to calculate formulas and retrieve and display information
from a variety of external sources, such as other documents,
other parts of the same document, or other applications. The
information in a field can be automatically updated.*

Insert Field

1. Place cursor where you want to insert a field.

2. Click **I**nsert, **F**ield .... [Alt] + [I] , [F]

*The **Field** dialog box displays.*

3. Click **C**ategories list box .... [Alt] + [C] , [↑] [↓]
   and select desired field category.

4. Click **Field n**ames list box........ [Alt] + [N] , [↑] [↓]
   and select field to insert.

   **To add specific switch, property,
   name, bookmark, or other instruction
   to selected field:**

   a. Click [**O**ptions...] .... [Alt] + [O]

   *Note: This function is enabled by default and is
            not available for certain **Numbering** and
            Equations and Formulas fields.*

   b. Select desired field instruction options.

5. Click **P**reserve Formatting .... [Alt] + [P]
   During Updates check box if desired. Leave
   check box empty to have Word update character
   formatting each time you update the field.

   *Note: This function is enabled by default and is
            not available for certain **Numbering** and
            Equations and Formulas fields.*

6. Click [**OK**   ] .... [↵]

114

Field Keyboard Shortcuts

To Insert:	Press:
Blank field	Ctrl + F9
DATE field	Alt + Shift + D
PAGE field	Alt + Shift + P
TIME field	Alt + Shift + T
LISTNUM field	Alt + Ctrl + L

To:	Press:
Lock field	Ctrl + F11
Go to next field	F11
Go to previous field	Shift + F11
Run a GOTOBUTTON or MACROBUTTON from field that displays the field results	Alt + Shift + F9
Switch between all field codes/results	Alt + F9
Switch between selected field code/result	Shift + F9
Unlink field	Shift + Ctrl + F9
Unlock field	Shift + Ctrl + F11
Update linked information in source document	Shift + Ctrl + F7
Update selected fields	F9

View Field Codes/Results

1. Select fields for which you want to switch display codes or results.

2. Point at field and click right mouse button.

3. Click **Toggle Field Codes/Results**.................. `T`
   from shortcut menu that appears.

FIND AND REPLACE

Allows you to find and replace text, graphics, fields, and special items in a document. You can also find and replace fonts, styles, and various other formatting attributes.

Find

> *Note:* *To quickly repeat the last search, press Shift+F4.*

1. Place cursor where you want to begin search.

2. Click **Edit, Find** .... `Alt`+`E`,`F`

   OR

   Press **Ctrl+F** .... `Ctrl`+`F`

*The **Find and Replace** dialog box displays.*

3. Click `Find` .... `Alt`+`D`

4. Click **Find What** box .... `Alt`+`N`, *text*
   and type text to search for.

   OR

   Click drop–down arrow `▼` in **Find What** .... `↑``↓`
   box to select from list of last four search entries.

5. Click `More ≉` .... `Alt`+`M`
   if desired, to display more **Find** options.

continued...

116

FIND (CONTINUED)

To search for special characters:

Click [Spe̲cial ▼] ...... [Alt]+[E], [↑] [↓], [↵]
and select special characters to find.

To search for formatting or formatted text:

a. Click [Fo̲rmat ▼] ... [Alt]+[O], [↑] [↓], [↵]
   and select formatting to find.

The dialog box for selected formatting item displays.

b. Select desired formatting options to find. *(See*
   ***CHARACTER FORMATTING**, page 101;*
   LANGUAGE**, page 230; **PARAGRAPH
   ***FORMATTING**, page 141; **STYLES**, page 146; and*
   ***TABS**, page 157.)*

Note: *You can search for formatting elements*
*without typing any text in **Find What** box in*
step 4. You can also select formatting in
***Find and Replace** dialog box by using the*
***Format** menu, or formatting shortcut keys.*

To clear all formatting from the Find dialog box:

Click [No Formatt̲ing] .... [Alt]+[T]

6. Click S̲earch box....................... [Alt]+[S], [↑] [↓]
   and select direction to search in.

7. Select additional search options from the following:

   • **Matc̲h Case** .... [Alt]+[H]

   • **Find Whole Words Onl̲y** .... [Alt]+[Y]

   • **U̲se wildcards** .... [Alt]+[U]

   • **Sounds li̲ke** .... [Alt]+[K]

   • **Find all word for̲ms** .... [Alt]+[M]

8. Click [F̲ind Next] .... [Alt]+[F]

Replace

1. Place cursor where you want to begin search.

2. Click **Edit**, **Replace**........................ [Alt]+[E],[E]

   OR

   Press **Ctrl+H**..................................... [Ctrl]+[H]

*The **Find and Replace** dialog box appears, displaying the **Replace** tab.*

3. Repeat steps 4–7 under **FIND**, page 115, to specify text or formatting to find.

4. Click **Replace with** box .... [Alt]+[I], *text* and type replacement text to insert.

   OR

   Click drop–down arrow [▼] in **Replace** ..... [↑] [↓] **with** box and select from list of the last four replacement entries.

   To replace with special characters:

   Click [**Special ▼**] ...... [Alt]+[E],[↑][↓],[↵] and select desired special characters.

   To replace with formatting or formatted text:

   a. Click [**Format ▼**] .... [Alt]+[O],[↑][↓],[↵] and select formatting to replace with.

   The dialog box for selected formatting item displays.

   b. Select desired formatting options to replace with. *(See **CHARACTER FORMATTING**, page 101; **LANGUAGE**, page 230; **PARAGRAPH FORMATTING**, page 141; **STYLES**, page 146; and **TABS**, page 157.)*

continued...

118

REPLACE (CONTINUED)

To clear all formatting from the Find dialog box:

Click | No Formatting | .... Alt + T

5. Click one of the following options:

- | **Find Next** | .... Alt + F

  to find next occurrence of information to
  be replaced.

- | **Replace** | .... Alt + R

  to replace occurrence with new information.

- | **Replace All** | .... Alt + A

  to replace all occurrences.

6. Click | **Cancel** | .... Esc

   to close **Find and Replace** dialog box.

FRAMES

*You can use frames in Word 97, but no longer need them to
wrap text around pictures and objects. In Word 97, you can
wrap text around an object in a document by using the
Format, **Picture** command, without first inserting it in a text
box or frame. (See **Wrap Text around Object**, page 176.)*

*Nor do you need frames any longer to position or size text or
graphics. Instead, Word 97 offers text boxes, which allow you
to position and size text and graphics in new, more interesting
ways. (See **Text Boxes**, page 178.)*

> Notes: Word 97 can still work with frames created
> in older versions of Word. Just use the
> **Frame** command under **Format**, **Frame**.

continued.

FRAMES (CONTINUED)

Frames are still necessary for positioning text or graphics that contain comments; notes; and certain fields, including tables of contents and table of contents entries, referenced documents, index entries, tables of authorities and table of authorities entries, and AUTONUM, AUTONUM GL, and AUTONUMOUT (used to number information in legal documents). See your online help for more information on positioning text/graphics that contain any of these items.

HEADING NUMBERING
*See **Format Multilevel List**, page 97.*

INSERT DATE AND TIME
Inserts current date and/or time in active document.

1. Place cursor in document where you want to insert current date or time.

2. Click **I**nsert, Date and **T**ime .... `Alt`+`I`,`T`

*The **Date and Time** dialog box displays.*

3. Select desired date or time format............. `↑``↓`
   from **A**vailable Formats list box.
   To set selected date or time as default format:

   a. Click | Default... | .... `Alt`+`D`

   b. Click | Yes | .... `↵`

4. Select the **U**pdate Automatically........... `Alt`+`U`
   check box to update the date periodically.

   *Note: Each time you want the date updated automatically, you must either print the document, or select the date and press **F9**.*

5. Click | OK | .... `↵`

MACROS

A **macro** is a shortcut to a series of commands that are performed automatically when the macro is run. You can create a macro by recording the steps of a complex task that you repeat often. Then run the macro each time you want the task performed, instead of performing the steps manually. For example, you can create a macro that automatically saves, prints, and then closes your document.

You can make a macro available to all documents or only to those based on a particular template. A macro can also be assigned to a shortcut key that makes it easier to run.

Create/Record Macro

Records a series of commands as a single command.

1. Click **Tools**, **Macro** .... `Alt`+`T`,`M`

2. Click **Record New Macro** .... `R`

*The **Record Macro** dialog box displays.*

3. Click **Macro name** box .... `Alt`+`M`, *name* and type macro name.

   Notes: Be sure the macro name you choose is unique. If two macros have the same name, Word will overwrite the commands of the existing macro with the commands of the new one.

              The first character in a macro name must be a letter. Remaining characters may be numbers, letters, or the underscore character. Spaces are not valid.

4. Click **Store macro in** box .... `Alt`+`S`, `↑` `↓` and select template/document to store macro in.

continued.

5. Click **D**escription box......... **Alt** + **D**, *description* and type description for macro.

    To store macro to a toolbar:

    a. Click **T**oolbars button .... **Alt** + **T**

*The **Customize** dialog box displays.*

    b. Click Commands .... **Alt** + **C**

    c. Click **Comman**d**s** box .... **Alt** + **D**

    d. Click macro you are recording and, holding the left mouse button, drag it to desired toolbar or menu.

    e. Click Close .... ↵ to close **Customize** dialog box and begin recording macro.

    To store macro to shortcut keys:

    a. Click **K**eyboard button .... **Alt** + **K**

*The **Customize Keyboard** dialog box displays.*

    b. Click **C**o**mm**ands list box..... **Alt** + **O**, **↑** **↓** and select macro you are recording.

    c. Click **Press** **n**ew shortcut key ... **Alt** + **N**, *keys* box and type desired key sequence.

    d. Click Close .... ↵ to close **Customize keyboard** dialog box and begin recording macro.

continued...

CREATE/RECORD MACRO (CONTINUED)

6. Click [OK] .... ⏎

*The **Record Macro** dialog box closes, and the **Macro**
toolbar displays, indicating that you can begin recording
macro:*

Stop R✕
■ ‖●

Cursor changes to: 📼

*(See your Word documentation or online Help for more
information on working with macros.)*

7. Perform functions to include in the macro.

*Macros will record menu and toolbar commands and options
executed using the mouse. Mouse movements, however, such as
moving the cursor or selecting, moving, and copying text, cannot
be recorded. You must perform these actions using the keyboard.*

   To pause recording:

   Click **Pause** button ‖●

8. Click **Stop** button ■ when finished performing
    desired commands and actions.

Create Macro Using Visual Basic

*You can also create a macro from scratch by using the Visual
Basic Editor. For more information on working with Visual
Basic in Word, see the **Microsoft Word Visual Basic
Reference** on the **Help Contents** tab for more information.*

1. a. Click <u>T</u>ools, <u>M</u>acro .... Alt + T , M

   b. Click **<u>M</u>acros** .... M

   OR

continued..

123

CREATE MACRO USING VISUAL BASIC (CONTINUED)

Press **Alt+F8**.............................. `Alt`+`F8`

*The **Macros** dialog box displays.*

2. Click **Macro Name** box............... `Alt`+`M`, *name*
   and type macro name.

   Note: Be sure the macro name you choose is
           unique. If two macros have the same
           name, Word will overwrite the commands
           of the existing macro with the commands
           of the new one.

3. Click **Macros in** box .... `Alt`+`A`, `↑` `↓`
   and select template or document
   to store Macro in.

4. Click [Create   ] .... `Alt`+`C`

*The **Visual Basic Editor** opens.*

5. Create Visual Basic macro code as desired.

Run Macro

1. a. Click **Tools**, **Macro** .... `Alt`+`T`, `M`

   b. Click **Macros** ....`M`

   OR

   Press **Alt+F8**............................. `Alt`+`F8`

*The **Macros** dialog box displays.*

2. Click **Macro Name** box............... `Alt`+`M`, *name*
   and type macro name.

3. Click [Run   ] .... `Alt`+`R`

Edit Macro

*You need a basic familiarity of Visual Basic to edit macros. Consult the **Microsoft Word Visual Basic Reference** on the **Help Contents** tab for more information.*

1. a. Click **T**ools, **M**acro .... `Alt`+`T`, `M`

    b. Click **M**acros .... `M`
    OR

    Press **Alt+F8** .... `Alt`+`F8`

*The **Macros** dialog box displays.*

2. Click **M**acro Name box .... `Alt`+`M`, *name*
    and type macro to edit.

    To access additional macros:

    Click M**a**cros in box .... `Alt`+`A`, `↑`, `↓`
    and select document or template from list.

3. Click [E̲dit   ] .... `Alt`+`E`

*The **Visual Basic Editor** opens.*

4. Edit Visual Basic macro code as desired.

Delete Macro

1. a. Click **T**ools, **M**acro .... `Alt`+`T`, `M`

    b. Click **M**acros .... `M`
    OR

    Press **Alt+F8** .... `Alt`+`F8`

*The **Macros** dialog box displays.*

2. Click **M**acro Name box .... `Alt`+`M`, `↑`, `↓`
    and type or select macro name.

3. Click [D̲elete   ] .... `Alt`+`D`

PAGE AND SECTION FORMATTING
Insert Breaks

INSERT BREAKS USING MENU

1. Position cursor where you want to insert break.

2. Click **Insert**, **Break**........................ Alt + I , B

*The **Break** dialog box displays.*

3. Select desired **Insert** break options:

   • **Page break**..................................... Alt + P
     to insert a manual page break.

   • **Column break** .... Alt + C
     to insert a manual column break.

4. Select desired **Section** break options:

   *Note: You can divide pages in a document into
   sections. A section is a portion of your
   document that is formatted differently from
   other sections of the document. For
   example, you can format headers and
   footers, page numbering, and newspaper–
   style columns differently in each section of
   a document. Until a new section break is
   inserted, Word treats the entire document
   as a single section.*

   • **Next page** .... Alt + N
     to insert a section break at the bottom of
     current page, so that new section starts at
     top of next page.

   • **Continuous**................................... Alt + T
     to insert a section break on current page
     without inserting a page break, so that new
     section starts immediately below previous.

continued...

126

INSERT BREAKS USING MENU (CONTINUED)

- **E**ven page .... `Alt`+`E`
  to insert a section break with new section
  starting on next even-numbered page.

- **O**dd page .... `Alt`+`O`
  to insert a section break with new section
  starting on next odd-numbered page.

5. Click `OK` .... `↵`

   Note: *You can also insert a column break with the*
   ***Fo**rmat,* ***C**olumns command. (See*
   ***Newspaper-Style Columns,** page 134.)*

INSERT BREAKS USING KEYBOARD

Formatting: **Press:**

Column break.................................. `Shift`+`Ctrl`+`↵`

Line break .... `Shift`+`↵`

Page break ....`Ctrl`+`↵`

Margins
SET MARGINS USING MENU

*Changes page margins in any screen view, using **Fi**le, **Page**
Setup command.*

1. Place cursor in document where you want to
   change margin settings, or select desired
   information with margins you want to change.

2. Double-click in blank area on horizontal or
   vertical ruler.

   Note: *The vertical ruler is only available in **Page**
   Layout and **Print Preview**.*

   OR

   Click **F**ile, **Page** Set**u**p .... `Alt`+`F`,`U`

continued..

SET MARGINS USING MENU (CONTINUED)

*The **Page Setup** dialog box displays.*

3. Click `Margins` .... `Alt`+`M`

4. Select **Mirror Margins** check box .... `Alt`+`I`
   to align margins for printing on
   both sides of a page.

5. Click in scroll box for margin you want to change:
   - **Top** .... `Alt`+`T`
   - **Bottom** .... `Alt`+`B`
   - **Left** .... `Alt`+`F`
     OR
   - **Inside** .... `Alt`+`N`
     (available only if **Mirror Margins** check
     box was selected in step 4).
   - **Right** .... `Alt`+`G`
     OR
   - **Outside** .... `Alt`+`O`
     (available only if **Mirror Margins** check
     box was selected in step 4).
   - **Gutter** .... `Alt`+`U`

6. Type desired margin width .... *number*
   in appropriate scroll box.

7. Repeats steps 5–6 to change additional margins.

8. Click one of the following to change how far
   headers and footers print from the edge of page:
   - **Header** .... `Alt`+`E`
   - **Footer** .... `Alt`+`R`
     *(See **Headers/Footers**, page 137.)*

continued...

128

SET MARGINS USING MENU (CONTINUED)

9. Click **Apply To** box........................ `Alt`+`A`, `↑` `↓`
   and select where to apply new margin(s).

   *Note: Choices vary depending on position of cursor in
   document and information selected in step 1.*

   **To use selected options as default settings
   for current document and all new documents
   based on current template:**

   a. Click `Default...` .... `Alt`+`D`

   b. Click `Yes` .... `↵`
      when confirmation dialog box appears.

   *Note: Selecting the **Default** button changes the
   defaults for options selected in the **Margins**
   tab as well as the other tabs in the **Page
   Setup** dialog box.*

10. Click `OK` .... `↵`

SET MARGINS USING MOUSE

*Changes page margins in **Print Preview** or **Page
Layout View** by dragging the mouse along the
horizontal and vertical rulers.*

1. Switch to Print Preview or Page Layout
   View. *(See **Page Layout View**, page 76,
   or **Print Preview**, page 77.)*

2. Place cursor over margin boundaries in vertical
   ruler to change top and bottom margins, or
   horizontal ruler to change left and right margins.

Mouse pointer changes to : ↔

3. Hold left mouse button.

4. Drag selected margin to new position.

5. Release mouse button.

Paper Size and Orientation

1. Place cursor in document or select desired pages with size and orientation to change.

2. Double–click on blank area of horizontal or vertical ruler.

   *Note: The vertical ruler is only available in **Page Layout View** and **Print Preview**.*

   OR

   Click **File, Page Setup** .... `Alt`+`F`,`U`

   *The **Page Setup** dialog box displays.*

3. Click `Paper Size` .... `Alt`+`S`

4. Click **Paper Size** box .... `Alt`+`R`,`↑``↓`
   and select a paper size.

   Note: Choices vary with different printers.

   To select custom paper size:

   a. Click **Width** box .... `Alt`+`W`, *number*
      and type desired paper width.

   b. Click **Height** box .... `Alt`+`E`, *number*
      and type desired paper height.

   *Note: Selecting custom paper width and height changes the **Paper Size** box to **Custom**.*

5. Select one of the following page orientations:

   • **Portrait** .... `Alt`+`I`

   • **Landscape** .... `Alt`+`C`

6. Click **Apply To** box .... `Alt`+`A`,`↑``↓`
   and select where to apply new paper size and orientation.

continued..

130

PAPER SIZE AND ORIENTATION (CONTINUED)

Note: *Choices vary depending on position of cursor in document and information selected in step 1.*

To use selected options as default settings for current document and all new documents based on current template:

a. Click **Default...** .... `Alt`+`D`

b. Click **Yes** .... `↵`

   when confirmation dialog box appears.

Note: *Selecting the **Default** button resets the defaults for all options in the **Page Setup** dialog box, including those on other tabs.*

7. Click **OK** .... `↵`

Paper Source

1. Place cursor in document, or select desired pages, with paper source you want to change.

2. Double–click in blank area of horizontal or vertical ruler.

   Note: *The vertical ruler is only available in **Page Layout View** and **Print Preview**.*

   OR

   Click **File**, Page Set**u**p .... `Alt`+`F`,`U`

*The **Page Setup** dialog box displays.*

3. Click **Paper Source** .... `Alt`+`P`

4. Click **First Page** list box .... `Alt`+`F`,`↑``↓`

   and select paper source for first page.

continued..

5. Click **Other Pages** list box .... `Alt`+`O`, `↑` `↓`
   and select paper source for pages
   other than the first.

6. Click **Apply To** box .... `Alt`+`A`, `↑` `↓`
   and select where to apply new paper source.

   *Note: Choices vary depending on position of
   cursor in document and information
   selected in step 1.*

   **To use selected options as default settings
   for current document and all new documents
   based on current template:**

   a. Click `Default...` .... `Alt`+`D`

   b. Click `Yes` .... `↵`
      when confirmation dialog box appears.

   *Note: Selecting the **Default** button resets the
   default options selected in the **Paper
   Source** tab, as well as the other tabs in the
   Page Setup dialog box.*

7. Click `OK` .... `↵`

Page Layout

1. Place cursor in document where you want to
   change layout, or select desired pages with layout
   you want to change.

2. Double–click in blank area of horizontal or vertical ruler.

   *Note: The vertical ruler is only available in **Page
   Layout View** and **Print Preview**.*

   OR

   Click **File**, **Page Setup** .... `Alt`+`F`, `U`

continued...

132

*The **Page Setup** dialog box displays.*

3. Click Layout .... Alt + L

4. Click **Section start** box .... Alt + R , ↑ ↓
   and select where to start current section.

5. Select one of the following **Headers and Footers** options:

   • **Different odd and even** .... Alt + O
     to create one header/footer for even–
     numbered pages and another for odd pages.

   • **Different first page** .... Alt + F
     to create a different header/footer for the
     first page of a section or document.

6. Click **Vertical Alignment** box .... Alt + V , ↑ ↓
   and select a vertical text alignment.

7. Click **Apply To** box .... Alt + A , ↑ ↓
   and select where to apply new layout options.

   *Note: Choices vary depending on position of cursor in
            document and information selected in step 1.*

   To add line numbers to the modified selection:

   a. Click Line Numbers... .... Alt + N

*The **Line Numbers** dialog box displays.*

   b. Select **Add line numbering** check box L
      if desired, to print line numbers in left
      margin of selection.

   c. Click **Start at** box .... Alt + A , *number*
      and type line to start numbering at.

continued.

133

d. Click **From text** box .... `Alt`+`T` , *number*
and type distance to place between
line numbers and document text.

e. Click **Count by** box .... `Alt`+`B` , *number*
and type increment to number
lines by (e.g., to print line numbers
2, 4, 6, etc., type **2**).

f. Select **Numbering** option:

- **Restart each page**................................. `P`
to restart line numbering (with the number
in the **Start at** box) on each new page.

- **Restart each section** .... `S`
to restart line numbering (with the number
in the **Start at** box) at the beginning of each
new section.

- **Continuous**.. `C`
to continue a single line numbering sequence
(starting with number in the **Start at** box)
throughout entire document.

g. Click | OK | .... `↵`

**To use selected options as default settings
for current document and all new documents
based on current template:**

a. Click | Default... | .... `Alt`+`D`

b. Click | Yes | .... `↵`
when confirmation dialog box appears.

*Note: Selecting the **Default** button resets the
defaults for options selected in all tabs in
the **Page Setup** dialog box.*

8. Click | OK | .... `↵`

134

Newspaper–Style Columns

CREATE NEWSPAPER COLUMNS USING MENU

*You must be in Page Layout View to insert newspaper–style columns. (See **PAGE LAYOUT VIEW**, page 76.)*

1. Place cursor in document and select desired information or section of column that you want to add or remove newspaper–style columns from.

2. Click **Format**, **Columns** .... `Alt`+`O`,`C`

*The **Columns** dialog box displays.*

3. Select one of the following column format options from **Presets**:

   - **One** .... `Alt`+`O`
     to insert one column.

   - **Two** .... `Alt`+`W`
     to insert two columns of equal width.

   - **Three** .... `Alt`+`T`
     to insert three columns of equal width.

   - **Left** .... `Alt`+`L`
     to insert two columns, with the left one–half as wide as the right.

   - **Right** .... `Alt`+`R`
     to insert two columns, with the right one–half as wide as the left.

continued..

CREATE NEWSPAPER COLUMNS USING MENU (CONTINUED)

OR

Click **Number of Columns** .... `Alt`+`N` , *number*
box and type number of columns to insert.

To change column width and spacing:

a. Click `OK` ....`↵`
to close **Columns** dialog box.

b. Click and drag column markers `🔲` in
horizontal ruler to desired spacing and width
positions.

OR

a. Deselect **Equal Column Width** .... `Alt`+`E`
check box.

b. Click in the **Width** box .... `Alt`+`I` , *number*
for the first column to modify and
type new width measurement.

c. Click in the **Spacing** box...... `Alt`+`S` , *number*
for the first column to modify and
type new spacing measurement.

d. Press **Tab** .... `Tab`
to move to **Width** and **Spacing** boxes for other
columns to change, and type desired new
measurements.

4. Click `OK` ....`↵`

136

CREATE NEWSPAPER COLUMNS USING MOUSE

Note: *To create columns of varying width, it is necessary to use the* ***F****ormat,* ***C****olumns command. (See* ***Newspaper–Style Columns****, page 134).*

You must be in Page Layout View to insert columns. (See ***PAGE LAYOUT VIEW****, page 76.)*

1. Place cursor in document and select desired information or section of column that you want to add or remove newspaper–style columns from.

   Note: *Newspaper–style columns are section-specific. Section breaks are inserted above and below any selected information.*

2. Click **Columns** button 🖽 in **Standard** toolbar.

3. Hold left mouse button and drag pointer over drop–down grid to select desired number of columns.

   To force the start of a new newspaper column:

   a. Place cursor at column break point.

   b. Click **I**nsert, **B**reak .... Alt + I , B

   c. Click **C**olumn break .... Alt + C

Text after cursor moves to the top of the next column.

   To remove newspaper columns:

   a. Click section, or select multiple sections, to remove columns from.

   b. Click **F**ormat, **C**olumns .... Alt + O , C

The ***Columns*** *dialog box displays.*

   c. Click 🖽 **O**ne .... Alt + O
      from column presets.

   d. Click [OK] .... ⏎

Headers/Footers
CREATE HEADER

1. Click **View**, **Header and Footer** ...... `Alt` + `V` , `H`

The ***Header*** *box displays along with the* ***Header and Footer*** *toolbar. Information in the body of the document is visible, but dimmed.*

2. Type desired header text in **Header** box.

    OR

    Click `Insert AutoText ▾` ..... `Alt` + `S` , `↑` `↓` , `↵`
    and select desired AutoText item to insert.

3. Select from the following toolbar options to insert desired header/footer fields:

🔲	***Insert Page Numbers***	*Inserts a PAGE field at the location of the cursor.*
🔲	***Format Page Number***	*Displays formatting options for Number, Chapter, or Page Numbering. (See* ***Insert Page Numbers***, *page 139.)*
🔲	***Insert Number of Pages***	*Inserts the total number of pages in document.*
🔲	***Insert Date***	*Inserts a* ***DATE*** *field at location of cursor.*
🔲	***Time***	*Inserts* ***TIME*** *field at location of cursor.*

4. Click `Close` .... `Alt` + `C`
    in **Header and Footer** toolbar.

138

CREATE FOOTER

1. Click 📑 on **Header and Footer** toolbar to move to the footer area.

2. Repeat steps 1–3 from **Create Header**, page 137.

   Note: *See **Page Layout**, page 131, for information on creating a different header and footer for just the first page of a section, or different odd– and even–numbered page headers and footers. Also see **Margins**, page 126, for information on changing the distance headers and footers print from the edge of the page.*

EDIT HEADER/FOOTER

You must be in Page Layout view or Print Preview to edit a header/footer.

1. Click **View**, **Header and Footer**....... `Alt` + `V`, `H`

*The **Header** box displays, along with the **Header and Footer** toolbar. Information in the body of the document is visible, but dimmed.*

2. Click **Switch between Header and Footer** 📑 in **Header and Footer** toolbar to switch between headers and footers.

   OR

   Click **Show Previous** 📑 in **Header and Footer** toolbar to move to previous header or footer.

   OR

   Click **Show Next** 📑 in **Header and Footer** toolbar to move to next header or footer.

3. Edit header or footer as desired.

continued..

EDIT HEADER/FOOTER (CONTINUED)

Note: You can double–click the dimmed header or footer to quickly switch between the two. Word will automatically change the same header or footer throughout the document.

To delete a header/footer:

a.   Select text/graphics in header/footer to delete.

b.   Press **Delete**...`Delete`

4.   Click `Close` ....`↵`

INSERT PAGE NUMBERS

1.   Click **Insert, Page Numbers** ....`Alt`+`I`,`U`

*The **Page Numbers** dialog box displays.*

2.   Click **Position** box ....`Alt`+`P`,`↑``↓`
     and select desired page number position.

3.   Click **Alignment** box.................`Alt`+`A`, `↑``↓`
     and select page number alignment.

*Note: Selecting **Inside** or **Outside** aligns page numbers close to the inside or outside edge of a page, if **Mirror Margins** option is selected in **Margins** tab of **Page Setup** dialog box. See **Margins**, page 126.)*

4.   Deselect **Show Number on First Page** ...`Alt`+`S`
     check box to suppress page numbers
     on first page of current section.

To change the page numbering format:

a.   Click `Format...` ....`Alt`+`F`

*The **Page Number Format** dialog box displays.*

continued...

140

b. Select **Include chapter number** .... `Alt`+`N`
check box to insert chapter number
along with the page number.

c. Click **Chapter starts with** ..... `Alt`+`P`, `↑` `↓`
style box and select heading style
that your chapter titles are formatted with.

Note: *The designated chapter heading style must
be used only for chapter titles. Do not
apply the same style to other text in
document.*

d. Click **Use separator** box ...... `Alt`+`E`, `↑` `↓`
and select the character to place
between chapter and page numbers.

e. Select one of the following **Page numbering**
options:

- Click **Continue from previous section** `Alt`+`C`
to continue the page numbering sequence
from the previous section.

   OR

- Click **Start at** .... `Alt`+`A`, *number*
and type page number to appear
on first page of selected sections.

f. Click [**OK**] .... `↵`

5. Click [**OK**] .... `↵`
to close **Page Numbers** dialog box.

PARAGRAPH FORMATTING
Format Paragraph Indents and Spacing
FORMAT PARAGRAPH INDENTS AND SPACING USING MENU

1. Place cursor in paragraph to format,
   or select multiple paragraphs.

2. Click **Format**, **Paragraph** .... `Alt`+`O`,`P`

   *The **Paragraph** dialog box displays.*

3. Click | Indents and Spacing | .... `Alt`+`I`

4. Click **Alignment** box .... `Alt`+`G`,`↑``↓`
   and select how to align selected
   paragraph in relation to indents.

5. Click **Outline level** box .... `Alt`+`O`,`↑``↓`
   if desired, to select the outline level to
   assign to selected paragraph(s).

6. a. Click in **Left** box .... `Alt`+`L`, *number*
      and type distance to place between
      the left margin and selected paragraph.

   b. Click in **Right** box .... `Alt`+`R`, *number*
      and type distance to place between
      the right margin and selected paragraph.

   OR

   a. Click **Special** box .... `Alt`+`S`,`↑``↓`
      and select a special indentation option:

      - Click **First line** to indent only the
        first line of paragraph.
      - Click **Hanging** to indent all lines
        in a paragraph except the first.

continued...

FORMAT PARAGRAPH INDENTS & SPACING USING MENU (CONT)

   b. Click **By** box........................ `Alt`+`Y`, *number*
and type special indent width.

7. Click **Before** .... `Alt`+`B`, *number*
and type distance to place between
selected paragraph and text above it.

8. Click **After**................................. `Alt`+`E`, *number*
and type distance to place between
selected paragraph and text below it.

9. Click **Line Spacing** box.............`Alt`+`N`, `↑` `↓`
and select a line spacing option.

**If you selected At Least, Exactly,
or Multiple in step 9:**

Click **At** box.............................. `Alt`+`A`, *number*
and type distance to place between
lines within selected paragraph.

To format tabs for the selected paragraphs:

   a. Click [**Tabs...**   ] ....`Alt`+`T`

*The **Tabs** dialog box displays.*

   b. Set tabs as desired. *(See **TABS**, page 157.)*

   c. Click [**OK**   ] ....`↵`
to close the **Tabs** dialog box.

10. Click [**OK**   ] ....`↵`
to close the **Paragraph** dialog box.

FORMAT PARAGRAPH INDENTS & SPACING USING TOOLBAR

Formatting: **Click:**

Left Align .... ▤

Center Align .... ▤

Right Align .... ▤

Justify .... ▤

Decrease Indent .... ▤

Increase Indent .... ▤

FORMAT PARAGRAPH INDENTS & SPACING USING MOUSE

1. Select paragraph(s) with indents to change.

2. Place mouse on top of desired indent marker:

   - **First Line Indent** .... ▽

   - **Left Indent** .... ⌂
     (select bottom marker)

   - **First Line and Left Indents simultaneously** ...... ⌛
     (select bottom marker)

   - **Right Indent** .... △

3. Hold left mouse button and drag to desired position.

4. Release mouse button.

144

PARAGRAPH INDENTS & SPACING SHORTCUT KEYS

Formatting:	Press:
Center Align	Ctrl + E
Double Spacing	Ctrl + 2
Hanging Indent	Ctrl + T
Justify	Ctrl + J
Left Align	Ctrl + L
Left Indent	Ctrl + M
Open/Remove One Line Before	Ctrl + 0 (Zero)
One-and-a-Half Line Spacing	Ctrl + 5
Remove Hanging Indent	Shift + Ctrl + T
Remove Left Paragraph Indent	Shift + Ctrl + M
Right Align	Ctrl + R
Single Spacing	Ctrl + 1

Text Flow

1. Place cursor in paragraph you want to format, or select multiple paragraphs.

2. Click **F**o**rmat**, **P**aragraph .... Alt + O , P

*The **Paragraph** dialog box displays.*

3. Click [Line and Page Breaks] .... Alt + P

4. Select from the following **Pagination** options:

   - **W**idow/Orphan Control .... Alt + W
     to prevent printing of single line/word at top of page.

continued.

145

- **Keep Lines Together**..........................Alt + K
  to prevent page breaks within paragraphs.

- **Keep with next**.................................Alt + X
  to prevent page breaks between selected
  paragraph and following.

- **Page break before** ....Alt + B
  to insert manual page break before
  selected paragraph.

5. Click **Suppress Line Numbers**...............Alt + S
   to suppress line numbers for selected
   paragraphs in sections formatted for line
   numbering.*(See **Page Layout**, page 131.)*

6. Click **Don't Hyphenate** ....Alt + D
   to prevent selected paragraphs from being
   hyphenated in files formatted for automatic
   hyphenation. *(See **HYPHENATION**, page 229.)*

   To format tabs for the selected paragraphs:

   a. Click [Tabs...] ....Alt + T

*The **Tabs** dialog box displays.*

   b. Set tabs as desired. *(See **TABS**, page 157.)*

   c. Click [OK] ....↵
      to close the **Tabs** dialog box.

7. Click [OK] ....↵
   to close the **Paragraph** dialog box.

STYLES

*Styles group a series of formatting elements into one function, and can be saved within a template or as part of a document. They can also be easily copied between different templates and documents using the **Organizer**. (See **Organizer**, page 68.)*

*The names of the available styles can be displayed at the left side of the document window by clicking on the **Styles** drop–down menu in the **Formatting** toolbar.*

Apply Styles

APPLY STYLE USING MENU

1. Select paragraphs you want to apply paragraph style to, or select characters you want to apply character style to.

2. Click **Format**, **Style** .... `Alt`+`O`, `S`

    *The **Style** dialog box displays.*

3. Click **List** box .... `Alt`+`L`, `↑` `↓`
    and select style options to display.

4. Click **Styles** list box .... `Alt`+`S`, `↑` `↓`
    and select style to apply.

    Note: Paragraph style names are bold; character styles are not bold.

5. Click ⎣ **Apply** ⎦ .... `Alt`+`A`

APPLY STYLE USING TOOLBAR

1. Select paragraphs to apply paragraph style to or select characters to apply character style to.

2. Click **Style** box `Normal ▾` .... `Shift`+`Ctrl`+`S`
    in **Formatting** toolbar.

3. Double–click style to apply from drop–down list.

STYLE KEYBOARD SHORTCUTS

Select paragraphs to apply paragraph style to, or select characters to apply character style to, and perform the following keystrokes to apply desired styles:

Command: | **Press:**

Apply current style.........................,..... `Shift` + `Ctrl` + `S`

Remove paragraph formatting .... `Ctrl` + `Q`
not part of applied style from
selected information

Start **AutoFormat**............................. `Alt` + `Ctrl` + `K`

Apply **Normal** *style ....* `Shift` + `Ctrl` + `N`

Apply **Heading 1** *style.......................* `Ctrl` + `Alt` + `1`

Apply **Heading 2** *style.......................* `Ctrl` + `Alt` + `2`

Apply **Heading 3** *style.......................* `Ctrl` + `Alt` + `3`

Apply **List** *style ....* `Shift` + `Ctrl` + `L`

Remove character styles from .... `Ctrl` + `Space`
selected characters

Create New Style

CREATE NEW STYLE USING MENU

1. Click **F**ormat, **S**tyle...................... `Alt` + `O`, `S`

   The **Style** *dialog box displays.*

2. Click [**N**ew...] .... `Alt` + `N`

   The **New Style** *dialog box displays.*

3. Click **N**ame box.............................. `Alt` + `N`, *text*
   and type new style name.

continued...

148

CREATE NEW STYLE USING MENU (CONTINUED)

4. Click **Style type** box.................. `Alt`+`T`, `↑` `↓`
   and select a style type.

5. Click **Based On** box................... `Alt`+`B`, `↑` `↓`
   and select style to base the new style on.

   *Note: By default, new paragraph styles are based
            on the style applied to the active paragraph.*

6. Click **Style for following** .... `Alt`+`S`, `↑` `↓`
   paragraph box and select style
   to apply to following paragraphs.

   *Note: This option is not available if **Character** was
            selected for **Style Type** in step 4.*

7. Click | Format ▼ | .... `Alt`+`O`, `↑` `↓`
   and select style element to format.

   Dialog box for selected style element displays.

8. Select formatting options for selected style
   element. (See **CHARACTER FORMATTING**, page
   101; **LANGUAGE**, page 230; **PARAGRAPH
   FORMTATTING**, page 141; **STYLES**, page 146; and
   TABS, page 157.)

9. Click | OK | .... `↵`

10. Repeat steps 7–9 to format additional style elements.

    To assign style to a shortcut key:

    a. Click | **Shortcut Key...** | .... `Alt`+`K`

    *The **Customize Keyboard** dialog box displays.*

    b. Click **Commands** list box ..... `Alt`+`O`, `↑` `↓`
       and select style to assign key
       sequence to.

continued.

149

c. Click **Press new shortcut key** ... `Alt`+`N`, *keys* box and type new key sequence.

Note: *If the selected keyboard sequence is already assigned to another command, that command will be displayed in the **Press new shortcut key** box.*

d. Click `Assign` ....`A` to assign new key sequence to selected style.

Note: *Clicking **Assign** overwrites any pre-existing command assignment for the selected shortcut keys with the current selection.*

e. Click `Close` ....`↵` to close **Customize keyboard** dialog box.

11. Select **Add to Template** check box.........`Alt`+`A` if desired, to add style to current template.

12. Select **Automatically update**..................`Alt`+`U` check box to modify style each time you apply manual formatting to a paragraph formatted in selected style. Also automatically changes all text formatted with affected style in active document.

13. Click `OK` ....`↵` to create new style and close **New Style** dialog box.

14. Click `Close` ....`Esc` to close **Style** dialog box.

150

CREATE STYLE USING TOOLBAR

1. Select text with formatting to include in style.

2. Click **Style** `Normal ▼` .... [Shift]+[Ctrl]+[S] , *text* box in **Formatting** toolbar and type new style name.

3. Press **Enter** .... [↵]

Modify Style

MODIFY STYLE USING MENU

1. Click **Format**, **Style** .... [Alt]+[O],[S]

*The **Style** dialog box displays.*

2. Click in **Styles** list box .... [Alt]+[S],[↑][↓] and select style to modify.

3. Click `Modify...` .... [Alt]+[M]

*The **Modify Style** dialog box displays.*

4. Follow steps 7–15 in **Create New Style Using Menu**, page 147.

MODIFY STYLE USING TOOLBAR

1. Make desired formatting changes to existing text containing style.

2. Click **Style** box `Normal ▼` .. [Shift]+[Ctrl]+[S] in **Formatting** toolbar.

3. Select style to modify .... [↑][↓]

4. Press **Enter** .... [↵]

*The **Reapply Style** dialog box displays.*

continued.

151

5.   Select **Redefine the style using** .... R
     the selected as an example?

     OR

     To reapply original style formatting:

     Select **Return the formatting of** .... S
     the selection to the style?

6.   Click [OK] .... ↵

Delete Style

> *Note: Built–in styles, such as heading level styles,
>   cannot be deleted.*

1.   Click **Format**, **Style** .... Alt + O , S

*The **Style** dialog box displays.*

2.   Click **List** box .... Alt + L , ↑ ↓
     and select style options to display.

3.   Click **Styles** list box .... Alt + S , ↑ ↓
     and select style you want to delete.

> *Note: Paragraph style names are bold; character
>   styles are not bold.*

4.   Click [**Delete**] .... Alt + D

5.   Click [Yes] .... ↵
     when **Delete Confirmation** dialog box appears.

6.   Click [Close] .... Esc

*The **Close** button displays after deletion is confirmed.*

Style Gallery

Copies styles from a different template to the current document template. The preview box displays different available template styles and previews what your document will look like when the new styles have been applied.

> *Note:* *Copying styles from the **Style Gallery** automatically overwrites styles in the document with the same style name.*

1. Click **Format, Style Gallery** .... `Alt`+`O`,`G`

*The **Style Gallery** dialog box displays.*

2. Click **Template** list box............`Alt`+`T`,`↑``↓` and select template with styles to copy.

3. Select one of the following **Preview** options:

   - **Document**.. `Alt`+`D`

   - **Example** .... `Alt`+`E`

   - **Style Samples** .... `Alt`+`S`

4. Click `OK` .... `↵` to close **Style Gallery** dialog box and apply styles from selected template.

AutoFormat

APPLY AUTOFORMAT

> *Note:* *This command does not format tables. To automatically format tables, use the **Table AutoFormat** command. (See **TABLE AUTOFORMAT**, page 192.)*

1. Place cursor anywhere in document to format entire document, or select desired information you want to format.

continued.

APPLY AUTOFORMAT (CONTINUED)

2. Click **F**or**mat**, **A**uto**Format**............ `Alt`+`O`,`A`

*The **AutoFormat** dialog box displays.*

3. Select from the following options:

   - Click **A**utoFormat now box .... `Alt`+`A`

   - Click AutoFormat and **r**eview each ...... `Alt`+`R`
     change box to display **AutoFormat** dialog
     box after each format change, so you
     can accept or reject each change.

4. Click **P**lease select a .... `Alt`+`P`,`↑``↓`
   document type to help the formatting
   process box and select document type to format.

5. Click ⌷ OK ⌷ .... `↵`

*Word automatically formats the document with styles from the
attached template. If you selected **AutoFormat and review
each change** in step 3, the **AutoFormat** dialog box
displays.*

6. Click ⌷ Accept All ⌷ .... `Alt`+`A`
   to accept all style changes.

   OR

   Click ⌷ **R**eject All ⌷ .... `Alt`+`R`
   to reject all style changes.

   To review individual style changes:

   a. Click ⌷ Review **C**hanges... ⌷ ...... `Alt`+`C`

*The **Review AutoFormat Changes** dialog box displays.*

continued...

154

b. Select from the following commands:

- **← Find** .... Alt + I

  to move to previous change.

- **Find →** .... Alt + F

  to move to next change.

- **Reject** .... Alt + R

  to reject current change.

- **Hide Marks** .... Alt + M

  to hide change marks and display
  document as it would look if all
  changes were accepted.

- **Undo** .... Alt + U

  to restore last changes you rejected.

c. Click **Close** .... Esc

  to exit **Review AutoFormat Changes** dialog box.

*The **AutoFormat** dialog box redisplays.*

To choose styles from different template:

*Note: See **STYLES**, page 146, for more
         information.*

a. Click **Style Gallery...** .... Alt + S

*The **Style Gallery** dialog box displays.*

b. Follow steps 2–4 under **Style Gallery**,
   page 152, to select desired style options.

AUTOFORMAT OPTIONS

1. Click **Format**, **AutoFormat** .... `Alt` + `O`, `A`

*The **AutoFormat** dialog box displays.*

2. Click | Options... | .... `Alt` + `O`

*The **AutoCorrect** dialog box displays.*

3. Click | AutoFormat |

4. Select parts of document to AutoFormat from following options:

   • **Hea<u>d</u>ings** .... `Alt` + `D`

   • **<u>L</u>ists** .... `Alt` + `L`

   • **A<u>u</u>tomatic bulleted lists** .... `Alt` + `U`

   • **Other <u>p</u>aragraphs** .... `Alt` + `P`

5. Select document elements to automatically replace from the following options:

   • **"Straight" <u>q</u>uotes with "smart quotes"** .. `Alt` + `Q`

   • **<u>O</u>rdinals (1st) with superscript** .... `Alt` + `O`

   • **<u>F</u>ractions (1/2) with fraction** .... `Alt` + `F`
     characters (½)

   • **Symbol characters with symbols** .... `Alt` + `Y`

   • ***<u>B</u>old * and _underline_** .... `Alt` + `B`
     with real formatting

   • **<u>I</u>nternet and network paths** .... `Alt` + `I`
     with hyperlinks

6. Select **<u>S</u>tyles** check box .... `Alt` + `S`
   if desired, to preserve styles already
   applied in a document.

continued...

AUTOFORMAT OPTIONS (CONTINUED)

7. Select **Plain text WordMail documents** .... `Alt`+`T`
   check box, if desired, to have Word always
   AutoFormat plain–text WordMail messages
   when you open them.

8. Click [OK] .... `↵`

AUTOFORMAT AS YOU TYPE

Applies AutoFormat to a document as you create it.

1. Click **Format**, **AutoFormat** .... `Alt`+`O`, `A`

*The **AutoFormat** dialog box displays.*

2. Click [Options...] .... `Alt`+`O`

*The **AutoCorrect** dialog box displays.*

3. Click [AutoFormat As You Type]

4. Follow steps 4–5 under **AutoFormat Options**
   to select desired automatic formatting and
   replacement to be performed as you type.

5. Select from the following **Always
   AutoFormat** options:

   - **Format beginning of list item** .... `Alt`+`M`
     like the one before it to have Word
     automatically repeat character formatting
     that you applied to first word or phrase in
     a list item to the next list item.

   - **Define styles based on your formatting** .... `Alt`+`S`
     to have Word automatically create new
     paragraph styles based on manual
     formatting that you apply to a document.

6. Click [OK] .... `↵`

TABS
Set Tab Stops
SET TAB STOPS USING MOUSE

1. Select paragraphs for which to set tab stops.

2. Drag tab marker ⌐⌐ on horizontal ruler to where you want to set the tab stop.

OR

Click **Tab Alignment** button at far left of horizontal ruler until desired tab stop button is visible:

*   **Left–aligned tab stop** .... `L`
*   **Center tab stop** .... `⊥`
*   **Right–aligned tab stop** .... `⌐`
*   **Decimal tab stop** .... `⊥`

3. Place mouse on new tab stop position in horizontal ruler.

4. Click left mouse button to set tab.

5. Repeat steps 2–4 to set additional tab stops for selected paragraphs.

SET TAB STOPS USING MENU

1. Select paragraphs for which to set tab stops.

2. Click **Format, Tabs** .... `Alt`+`O`,`T`

*The **Tabs** dialog box displays.*

3. Click **Tab Stop Position** box ..... `Alt`+`T`, *number* and type desired tab stop position.

4. Select one of the following **Alignment** options:

*   **Left** .... `Alt`+`L`
*   **Center** .... `Alt`+`C`

continued...

158

- **Right**.. `Alt`+`R`

- **Decimal** .... `Alt`+`D`

- **Bar**... `Alt`+`B`

5. Select one of the following **Leader** options:

- **1 None** `Alt`+`1`
  to leave space left of tab stop blank.

- **2**... `Alt`+`2`
  to fill space left of tab stop with ellipses.

- **3** --- `Alt`+`3`
  to fill space left of tab stop with a dashed line.

- **4** `Alt`+`4`
  to fill space left of tab stop with a solid line.

6. Click **Set** .... `Alt`+`S`

7. Repeat steps 3–6 to set additional tab stops.

8. Click **OK** .... `↵`

Set Default Tab Stops

> *Note:*   *Default tab stops cannot be set for individual paragraphs, only for an entire document or section.*

1. Click **Format**, **Tabs** .... `Alt`+`O`,`T`

*The **Tabs** dialog box displays.*

2. Click **Default Tab Stops** box .... `Alt`+`F`, *number* and type desired default tab.

3. Click **OK** .... `↵`

Remove Tab Stops

REMOVE TAB STOPS USING MOUSE

1. Select paragraphs to remove tab stops from.

2. Position pointer over tab stop ⌐ you want to remove in horizontal ruler.

3. Click and drag mouse down to pull tab marker off of ruler.

4. Release mouse button.

5. Repeat steps 2–4 to delete additional tab stops for selected paragraphs.

REMOVE TAB STOPS USING MENU

1. Select paragraphs to remove tab stops from.

2. Click **Format**, **Tabs** .... `Alt` + `O` , `T`

    *The **Tabs** dialog box displays.*

3. Click **Tab Stop Position** box ..... `Alt` + `T` , `↑` `↓` and select tab stop to remove.

4. Click `Clear` .... `Alt` + `E`

5. Repeat steps 3–4 to remove additional tab stops.

    OR

    Click `Clear All` .... `Alt` + `A` to remove all tab stops.

6. Click `OK` .... `↵`

PICTURES AND OTHER OBJECTS

In Word 97, you can draw objects, such as text boxes, AutoShapes, lines, and arrows, directly in a document. Or you can import objects created in other applications, such as clip art or WordArt.

AUTOSHAPES & FREEFORM DRAWINGS

*Word contains over 100 AutoShapes that you can insert and adjust using the **Drawing** toolbar. Or you can draw your own shapes using the freeform command on the **Drawing** toolbar.*

Draw AutoShape

1. a. Click **I**nsert, **P**icture.................. `Alt`+`I`, `P`

    b. Click **A**utoShapes .... `A`

    OR

    Click `AutoShapes ▾` .... `Alt`+`U`
    in **Drawing** toolbar.

2. Select an AutoShape category .... `↑` `↓`, `↵`

3. Select AutoShape.................. `↑` `↓` `→` `←`, `↵`
    to insert from drop–down grid.

Pointer changes to: ╋

   To insert default–size shape:
   Click in document where you want shape inserted.

   To custom size shape:
   a. Point to area where a corner of object will begin.

   b. Drag to desired size.

   Note: *To keep the shape's width–to–height ratio consistent, press the **Shift** key while dragging to size the shape.*

Draw Freeform Shape

1. a. Click **I**nsert, **P**icture.................. `Alt`+`I`, `P`

    b. Click **A**utoShapes .... `A`

    OR

continued.

DRAW FREEFORM SHAPE (CONTINUED)

Click | AutoShapes ▾ | .... Alt + U
in **Drawing** toolbar.

2. Click **Lines** 🖾 .... Alt + U , L

3. Select **Freeform** 🅖 from drop–down grid.

Pointer changes to: +

4. Draw shape as desired.

Drawing Toolbar

*The **Drawing** toolbar displays by default. If you have hidden it, however, it will automatically redisplay when you insert an AutoShape or freeform shape. The **Drawing** tool buttons and their corresponding commands are as follows:*

| Draw ▾ | **Drawing Menu**. Click to edit, change, combine or format drawing objects. |

| ▷ | **Select object** button. Click and drag to select multiple objects at one time. |

| ⟳ | **Free rotate** button. Click to rotate drawing object in any direction. |

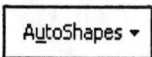

| AutoShapes ▾ | **AutoShapes** button. Click to select a ready-made shape (e.g., a line, basic shape, flowchart element, star, banner, or callout. |

| \ | **Line** button. Click and drag to insert line into document. |

| ↘ | **Arrow** button. Click and drag to insert arrow into document. |

| ▢ | **Rectangle** button. Click and drag to insert rectangle AutoShape into document. |

continued…

162

Oval button. Click and drag to insert oval AutoShape in document.

Text box button. Click and drag to insert text box. (See **TEXT BOXES**, page 178.)

Insert WordArt button. Click to display WordArt Gallery. (See **WORDART**, page 183.)

Fill color button. Click to select fill effect to add to object. (See **OBJECT FORMATTING**, page 167.)

Line color button. Click to select line color to add to object.

Font color button. Click to select a font text color.

Line style button. Click to select a line style.

Dash style button. Click to select a border dash style.

Arrow style button. Click to select arrow style.

Shadow button. Click to select a shadow style to add to object.

3–D button. Click to select a special 3-D effect to add to object.

Change Shape of Freeform Drawing

1. Click on desired freeform object to select it.

2. Click `Draw ▾` in **Drawing** toolbar .... Alt + R , E and select **Edit Points** from pop–up menu.

3. Position cursor on border of shape until cursor changes to: ✛

4. Click and drag to add new vertex (handle) position and reshape object.

Add Text to AutoShape or Freeform Drawing

1. Right–click on shape.

2. Select **Add Te__x__t** from shortcut menu............... X

3. Type text.. *text*

   Note: Text added to shape becomes part of the
   shape and moves with it. However, it will
   not rotate when shape is rotated. You can
   rotate text in shape using the Text
   Direction command on the Format menu.

   ### To edit text in AutoShape or Freeform Object:

   a. Right–click shape.

   b. Select **Edit Te__x__t** from shortcut menu............ X

   c. Edit text as desired.

Format AutoShape or Freeform Drawing

*See **OBJECT FORMATTING**, page 167.*

CLIP ART
Insert Clip Art

1. Click __I__nsert, __P__icture .... Alt + I , P

*The **Insert Picture** dialog box displays.*

2. Click __C__lip Art C

*The **Microsoft Clip Gallery** opens.*

3. Select a Clip Art category .... ↑ ↓
   from list on left side of **Clip Art** tab to display
   related art on the right side.

Each category shows different Clip Art. Word displays the
keywords used to find images in the selected category at the
bottom of the dialog box.

4. Double-click image to insert.

continued...

164

INSERT CLIP ART (CONTINUED)

To Find Clip Art in Clip Gallery:

a. Click `Find...` .... `Alt` + `F`
   in the **Clip Art** tab.

b. Click **Keywords** box .... `Alt` + `K` , *text*
   and type one–word description.

c. Click `Find Now` .... `Alt` + `F`

*Closes the **Find Clip** dialog box and displays Clip Art relating to the keyword in the **Microsoft Clip Gallery** dialog box.*

5. Repeat steps 1–3 until you find desired art.

Format Clip Art Image

*See **OBJECT FORMATTING**, page 167.*

IMPORTED PICTURES

Insert Picture from File

Inserts a picture created in another application.

1. Position cursor where picture will be inserted.

2. Click **Insert**, **Picture** .... `Alt` + `I` , `P`

3. Click **From File** .... `F`

*The **Insert Picture** dialog box appears.*

4. Select **Float over text** check box .... `Alt` + `L`
   to insert a floating picture that you can
   position by dragging. Deselect to insert
   picture directly in text on same line as
   surrounding text (inline graphic).

5. Select **Link to File** check box .... `Alt` + `K`
   if desired, to maintain link between picture and
   its source file. If you edit source file, changes
   are updated in linked picture.

6. Double–click file to insert.

Create and Import Picture

1. Position cursor where picture will be inserted.

2. Click **Insert**, **Object**........................ Alt + I , O

3. Click **Create new** .... Alt + N

4. Click **Object type** list .... Alt + T , ↓ ↑
    and select type of object to insert.

5. Click OK .... ↵

The selected application opens.

6. Create and save picture in source application.

Picture Toolbar

*The **Picture** toolbar automatically appears when you insert or select a picture, displaying the following buttons and commands:*

Insert picture *button. Click to insert picture from file.*

Image control *button. Click to select image appearance (Automatic, Grayscale, Black & White, or Watermark).*

More contrast *button. Click to increase the contrast (intensity) of colors in picture.*

Less contrast *button. Click to reduce contrast (intensity) of colors in picture.*

More brightness *button. Click to lighten selected picture colors.*

Less brightness *button. Click to darken selected picture colors.*

continued...

166

PICTURE TOOLBAR (CONTINUED)

Crop button. Click button and drag pointer over picture to crop.

Line style button. Click to select line width.

Text wrapping button. Click to select format when wrapping text around image (object).

Format object button. Click to format line, color, fill, position, size, and other properties of picture.

Set transparent color button. Click to make bitmap color transparent, rather than opaque.

Reset picture button. Click to undo all image edits.

Crop Picture

CAUTION: Do not confuse cropping with resizing a picture. Cropping trims the picture.

1. Select picture to crop.

*The **Picture** toolbar displays.*

2. Click **Crop** in the **Picture** toolbar.

The cursor changes to cropping tool:

3. Position cropping tool on selected picture handle.

    Note: The cropping tool only crops in a square or rectangular shape at 45° angles.

4. Drag cursor across picture to crop.

5. Press **Escape** to exit Crop mode..................... Esc

    *Note: Word retains original uncropped picture. To undo cropping, follow **Restore Picture** procedure, below.*

Restore Picture

Restores modified pictures to their original state. Undoes cropping, color, and size modifications, etc.

1. Select picture to restore.

*The **Picture** toolbar displays.*

2. Click **Reset Picture** 🖼 in the **Picture** toolbar.

Format Picture

*See **OBJECT FORMATTING**, below.*

OBJECT FORMATTING

Resizes, changes line style and borders, adds shading to text boxes, imported pictures, AutoShapes, etc.

Group/Ungroup Text and/or Objects

Groups objects with text and/or other objects, so that they can be moved, edited, copied, etc., as a single unit.

1. Hold down **Shift** and click each text box, object, and/or segment of text to group, one at a time.

2. Click in ⌈ Draw ▾ ⌉ in **Drawing**.......... **Alt** + **R** , **G** toolbar and select **Group** from pop–up list.

    To ungroup a grouped set:

    Click ⌈ Draw ▾ ⌉ in **Drawing** .... **Alt** + **R** , **U** toolbar and select **Ungroup** from pop–up list.

Move Object

1. Select object(s) to move.

2. Drag object to new location.

3. Click outside the object to deselect it.

168

Delete Object

1. Select object to delete.
2. Press the **Delete** key... `Delete`

Align or Distribute Objects

1. Press **Shift** and click each object to align.
2. Click `Draw ▾` .... `Alt`+`R`
3. Click **Align or Distribute** .... `A`
4. Select desired alignment option.

Resize Object

1. Select object.
2. Drag handles to size.

   OR

   Press **Shift** and drag handle to maintain proportions (aspect ratio) of object and avoid distortion.

   OR

   Press **Ctrl** and drag handle to resize object from center.

   OR

   Press **Ctrl+Shift** and drag handle to resize object proportionally from its center.

   OR

   a. Click **Format** .... `Alt`+`O`
      and select object type to resize.

*The **Format** dialog box displays.*

   b. Click `Size`

   c. Click **Height** box .... `Alt`+`E`, *number* and type desired object height.

continued..

d. Click **Wi_d_th** box .... `Alt`+`D`, *number*
   and type desired object width.

e. Click `⎡  OK  ⎤` .... `↵`

OR

a. Click **Height** box .... `Alt`+`H`, *number*
   beneath **Scale** and type desired
   percentage of original object height.

b. Click **Width** box .... `Alt`+`W`, *number*
   beneath **Scale** and type desired
   percentage of original object width.

c. Click `⎡  OK  ⎤` .... `↵`

3. Press **Shift** and double–click .... `Shift`
   any handle to return object to original
   aspect ratio (proportion) after resizing.

*The picture remains sized but will be proportionally defined by
reducing the distorting extension.*

Flip Object

*Some objects cannot be flipped, for example, bitmaps (most
Clip Art images are bitmaps).*

1. Select object(s) to flip.

2. Click `Draw ▼` in **Drawing** toolbar .... `Alt`+`R`

3. Click **Rotate or Fli_p_** .... `P`

4. Click **Flip _H_orizontal** .... `H`

   OR

   Click **Flip _V_ertical** .... `V`

Rotate Object Left/Right

*Rotates object 90°. To rotate to any angle, see **Rotate Freely**, below.*

1. Select object(s) to rotate.
2. Click `Draw ▾` in **Drawing** toolbar .... Alt + R
3. Click **Rotate or Flip**.. P
4. Click **Rotate Right** .... R

   OR

   Click **Rotate Left**.. L

Rotate Freely

1. Select object to rotate.
2. Click **Free Rotate** 🔄 in **Drawing** toolbar.

Cursor changes shape to:

3. Drag object handle to rotate.

   Notes: *To control the rotation and limit it to 45°*
   *angles, press **Shift** and drag.*

   To rotate object using opposite handle as
   *anchor, press **Ctrl** and drag.*

Arrange Stacked Objects

1. Select object.

   Note: *If object is hidden in the stack, press **Tab***
   *or **Shift+Tab** to select it.*

2. Click `Draw ▾` in **Drawing** toolbar .... Alt + R
3. Click **Order**... R
4. Select **Bring Forward**.. F
   to bring object up one layer.

   OR

   Select **Send Backward**.. B
   to send object back one layer.

continued.

171

OR

Select **Bring to Front**..T
to place object on top of stack.

OR

Select **Send to Back**...K
to send object to bottom of stack.

Add Shadow or 3D Effect to Object

1. Select object.

2. Click **Shadow** ▪ or **3D Effect** ▪ button
   on **Drawing** toolbar and select desired
   effect from pop–up list.

   Note: *To remove shadow or 3D effect, click No*
   Shadow in pop–up list.

Change Border Color

Note: *Word automatically adds a border around a*
text box when you create it. To omit
border, select No Line in step 5 below.

1. Click object to select it.

2. Click **Format**.....................................Alt + O
   and select type of object to add border color to.

*The **Format** dialog box displays.*

3. Click [Colors and Lines]

4. Click **Color** box beneath **Line** ....Alt + O

5. Select desired border color ... ↑ ↓ ← → ,↵
   from drop–down color grid.

6. Click [OK] ....↵

172

Remove Object Border

1. Open **Format** dialog box, if not already open. *(See steps 1–2 in **Change Border Color**, page 171.)*

2. Click `Colors and Lines`

3. Click **Co̲lor** box beneath **Line**.................. `Alt`+`O`

4. Click `          No Line          ` .... `↑`,`↵`
   from drop–down color grid.

5. Click `     OK     `

Change Border Styles

1. Open **Format** dialog box, if not already open. *(See steps 1–2 in **Change Border Color**, page 171.)*

2. Click `Colors and Lines`

3. Click **S̲tyle** box................... `Alt`+`S`,`↑`,`↓`,`↵`
   and select a border width and style.

4. Click **D̲ashed** box.............. `Alt`+`D`,`↑`,`↓`,`↵`
   and select a dashed border style, if desired.

   OR

   To add a pattern to border:

   a. Click **Co̲lor** beneath **Line**.................... `Alt`+`O`

   b. Click **P̲atterned Lines** .... `Alt`+`P`
      from drop–down color grid.

   *The **Patterned Lines** dialog box opens.*

   c. Click in **Pa̲ttern** ...... `Alt`+`T`,`↑`,`↓`,`←`,`→`
      window and select a pattern style.

   d. Click **F̲oreground** box .... `Alt`+`F`

continued.

173

e. Select desired foreground ... ⬆ ⬇ ⬅ ➡ , ↵
   color from drop–down color grid.

f. Click **Background** box....................... Alt + B

g. Select a background.......... ⬆ ⬇ ⬅ ➡ , ↵
   color from drop–down color grid.

h. Click | OK | .... ↵

5. Click **Weight** box...................... Alt + W , *number*
   and type custom border width, if desired.

6. Click | OK | .... ↵

Shade Object Contents

1. Display **Format** dialog box, if not already open.
   *(See steps 1–2 in **Change Border Color**, page 171.)*

2. Click | Colors and Lines |

3. Click **Color** box beneath **Fill** .... Alt + C

4. Select desired fill color.......... ⬆ ⬇ ⬅ ➡ , ↵

5. Select **Semitransparent** check box,
   if desired, to fill object with semitransparent,
   rather than opaque, shading.

   *Note: This option is not available if object fill has
   been formatted with a gradient, texture,
   pattern, or picture fill effect. (See **Add Fill
   Effects to Object**, page 174, for more
   information.)*

6. Click | OK | .... ↵

Remove Object Shading

1. Display **Format** dialog box, if not already open.
   (See steps 1–2 in Change Border Color, page 171.)

2. Click | Colors and Lines |

3. Click **C**olor box beneath **Fill**.................. `Alt`+`C`

4. Click | No Fill | .... `↑`, `↵`
   from drop–down grid.

5. Click | OK |

Add Fill Effects to Object

1. Display **Format** dialog box, if not already open.
   (See steps 1–2 in Change Border Color, page 171.)

2. Click | Colors and Lines |

3. Click **C**olor box beneath **Fill**............ `Alt`+`C`, `F`
   and select **F**ill Effects from drop–down grid.

*The **Fill Effects** dialog box appears.*

To add gradient to object background:

Follow steps 3–7 under **Add Gradient to Background Color**, page 87.

To add texture to object background:

Follow steps 2–4 under **Add Texture to Background**, page 88.

To add a pattern to object background:

Follow steps 2–8 under **Add a Pattern to Background**, page 89.

To add a picture to object background:

Follow steps 2–5 under **Add a Picture to Background**, page 89.

Position Object

1. Select object.
2. Drag to desired location.

   OR

   a. Click **F**ormat............................... `Alt`+`O`
      and select object type to position.

   b. Click [Position]

   c. Click **H**orizontal box............. `Alt`+`H`, *number*
      and type a position for left
      edge of object.

   d. Click **F**rom........................... `Alt`+`F`, `↑``↓`
      and select a page element to
      horizontally position object in
      relation to (**Margin**, **Page**, or **Paragraph**).

   e. Click **V**ertical box................ `Alt`+`V`, *number*
      and type a position for top of object.

   f. Click F**r**om........................... `Alt`+`R`, `↑``↓`
      and select a page element to
      vertically position object in relation
      to (**Margin**, **Page**, or **Paragraph**).

3. Select **M**ove object with text check........ `Alt`+`M`
   box to have object move with the text
   it is anchored to; deselect to have object
   anchor to remaining text closest to
   it when original anchored text is moved.

4. Select **L**ock anchor............................... `Alt`+`L`
   to have object always stay on page it
   was created on.

5. Click [**OK**] .... `↵`

Wrap Text Around Object

Wraps text on page around object.

1. Select object.

2. Click **Format** .... Alt + O
   and select object type to wrap text around.

*The **Format** dialog box displays.*

3. Click Wrapping

4. Select desired Wrapping style from the following:

- **Square** .... Alt + Q
  to wrap text in a square around all sides of object.

- **Tight**.................................. Alt + T
  to conform wrapping to shape of object.

- **Through**............................. Alt + H
  to conform wrapping to shape of object,
  as well as to wrap inside any blank spaces
  within object.

- **None** .... Alt + N
  to omit wrapping.

- **Top and bottom** .... Alt + O
  to wrap text around top and bottom borders
  of object, but not on sides.

continued

WRAP TEXT AROUND OBJECT (CONTINUED)

5. Select desired sides to wrap around:

- **B**oth Sides........................ `Alt`+`B`
  to wrap text around left and right sides of object.

- **L**eft.................................... `Alt`+`L`
  to wrap text on the left side of object.

- **R**ight.................................. `Alt`+`R`
  to wrap text around the right side of object.

- La**r**gest Side .... `Alt`+`A`
  to wrap text around the side of the object
  (right or left) with the most space.

6. Click **To**p box............................ `Alt`+`P`, *number*
   and type distance to place between
   wrapped text and top of object.

7. Click **Botto**m box........................ `Alt`+`M`, *number*
   and type distance to place between
   wrapped text and bottom of object.

8. Click **Le**ft box .... `Alt`+`F`, *number*
   and type desired distance between
   wrapped text and left edge of object.

9. Click **Right** box............................ `Alt`+`G`, *number*
   and type desired distance between
   wrapped text and right edge of object.

10. Click **OK** .... `↵`

TEXT BOXES

In Word 97, text boxes replace the frames used in earlier versions of Word. Use text boxes to position or offset text on a page, flow text from one part of a document to another, wrap text around a graphic, or manipulate text as a graphic element.

Create Text Box

1. Click **I**nsert, Te**x**t Box...................... Alt + I , X
   OR
   Click **Text Box** button 🔳 on **Drawing** toolbar.

Screen switches to Page Layout View, and pointer changes to: +

2. Click where top–left corner of text box should begin and drag down to where the bottom–right corner should stop.

3. Release mouse button.

*The **Text Box** floating toolbar displays.*

4. Type desired text in text box.
   Note: Text in text box wraps automatically.
   OR
   Click **T**able, **I**nsert Table .... Alt + A , I
   to create new table in text box.
   OR
   Click **I**nsert .... Alt + I , P or O
   and click graphic to place in text box, such as **P**icture or **O**bject.

   *Note: AutoShapes and WordArt must be grouped with their text box after insertion. Otherwise they behave as page elements, rather than text box elements, and cannot be moved or manipulated together with text box. See **Group/Ungroup Objects and/or Objects**, page 167.*

Select Text Box

Click text box border.

*When text box is selected, **Text Box** floating toolbar displays, pointer changes to crossbar, and handles and border appear around text box:*

Select Object in Text Box

Click on object inside text box.

When object in text box is selected, handles appear around object:

Format Text Box

*See **OBJECT FORMATTING**, page 167.*

Format Text in a Text Box

1. Select text to format.

2. Use character and paragraph formatting procedures to format text as desired. *(See **CHARACTER FORMATTING**, page 101; **LANGUAGE**, page 230; **PARAGRAPH FORMATTING**, page 141; **STYLES**, page 146; and **TABS**, page 157.)*

Rotate Text in a Text Box

1. Select text box.

2. Display **Text Box** floating toolbar. *(See **TOOLBARS**, page 82.)*

3. Click **Change Text Direction** button on **Text Box** floating toolbar.

4. Repeat step 3 as desired to rotate another 90°.

Set Margins for Text Box

1. Select text box.

2. Click **F̲ormat**, **Text B̲ox** .... `Alt`+`O`,`O`

*The **Format Text Box** dialog box displays.*

3. Click `Text Box`

4. Click **L̲eft** ....`Alt`+`L`
   and type distance to place between
   text and left text box border.

5. Click **R̲ight**...`Alt`+`R`
   and type distance to place between
   text and right text box border.

6. Click **T̲op**...`Alt`+`O`
   and type distance to place between
   text and top text box border.

7. Click **B̲ottom** ....`Alt`+`B`
   and type distance to place between
   text and bottom text box border.

8. Click `OK` ....`↵`

Link Text Boxes

Connects text boxes, so that their contents flow from one text box to the next throughout the chain.

1. Select first text box.

2. Display **Text Box** floating toolbar.
   *(See **TOOLBARS**, page 82.)*

3. Click **Create Text Box Link** button `⊂⊃`
   on **Text Box** floating toolbar.

continued..

181

4. Click in empty text box to link to.

Pointer changes to: ✍ when positioned over text box to link to.

5. Repeat steps 2–4 to link all text boxes in chain.

   To remove link between text boxes:

   a. Select the first of the linked text boxes.

   b. Click **Break Forward Link** button 🔗 in **Text Box** floating toolbar.

Move between Linked Text Boxes

Moves to next/previous box in chain of linked text boxes.

1. Select text box.

2. Display **Text Box** floating toolbar. *(See TOOLBARS, page 82.)*

3. Click **Next Text Box** 🔲 in **Text Box** floating toolbar.

   OR

   Click **Previous Text Box** 🔲 in **Text Box** floating toolbar.

WATERMARK

Add Watermark

Adds a graphic or text as a watermark.

1. Click **View**, **Header and Footer** ...... `Alt`+`V`,`H`

*The **Header and Footer** window opens.*

2. Click **Show/Hide Document Text** 📄 on the **Header and Footer** toolbar.

continued...

ADD WATERMARK (CONTINUED)

To insert a graphic or other object for use as watermark:

a. Click **I**nsert, **P**icture .... `Alt` + `I` , `P`

b. Select type of graphic to insert.

c. Double–click art or file to insert.

Note: *For more information, see* **AUTOSHAPES & FREEFORM DRAWINGS**, *page 160, and* **IMPORTED PICTURES**, *page 164.*

To insert text for use as watermark:

a. Click **I**nsert, Te**x**t Box .... `Alt` + `I` , `X`

b. Drag to create text box.

c. Type text in box.

d. Click outside text box.

Note: *For more information on text boxes, see* **TEXT BOXES**, *page 178.*

3. Click object to convert to watermark.

4. Drag selected object to position it.

5. Resize selected object by dragging a sizing handle if desired.

6. Right–click on object to display shortcut menu.

7. Click **Format** P**i**cture, **O**bject, ... `I` / `O` or **Text Bo**x.

The **Format** *dialog box appears.*

8. Click [Wrapping]

9. Set **Wrapping Style** to **N**one .... `Alt` + `N`

10. Click [Picture]

continued..

11. Click **C**olor box and select .... `Alt`+`C`, `↓`
    Watermark from drop–down list.

12. Click [OK] .... `↵`

13. Click [Close] on **Header and Footer** toolbar ... `Alt`+`C`

Format a Watermark

*See **OBJECT FORMATTING**, page167x.*

WORDART

Create WordArt Picture

Applies special effects to text in active document.

1. Select text to create picture from.

2. Click **I**nsert, **P**icture .... `Alt`+`I`, `P`, `W`
    WordArt.

*The **WordArt Gallery** dialog box displays.*

3. Double–click desired WordArt style.

*The **Edit WordArt Text** dialog box displays.*

4. Edit text selected in step 1, if desired, or type new text.

5. Click [OK] .... `↵`

*The **WordArt** toolbar displays.*

6. Drag WordArt to position it if desired.

7. Use **WordArt** toolbar to edit object as desired.

   Note: To display WordArt toolbar at any time,
           click on WordArt object.

Format WordArt Picture

*See **OBJECT FORMATTING**, page 167.*

184

TABLES
CREATE TABLES
Convert Text to Table

Converts existing paragraphs to table, allowing you to determine the number of columns and rows, column widths, and column separator characters.

> *Note: In addition to using the following steps, you can also quickly convert text to table by selecting the desired information and clicking the **Insert Table** button in the **Standard** toolbar, or by selecting **Insert Table** from the **Table** menu. Word automatically decides where to insert columns and rows into the selected text.*

1. Select paragraphs you want to convert to a table.

2. Click T**a**ble, Con**v**ert Text to Table.... `Alt`+`A`,`V`

*The **Convert Text to Table** dialog box displays.*

3. Click **Number of columns** box ... `Alt`+`C`, *number* and type desired number of columns.

> *Note: Word selects the most logical number of columns based on the selected information.*

4. Click **Number of rows** box .... `Alt`+`R`, *number* and type desired number of rows.

> *Note: Word selects the most logical number of rows based on the selected information.*

5. Click **Column width** box........... `Alt`+`W`, *number* and type column width (default is **Auto**).

continued.

6. Select text to convert to column markers in the
   Separate Text At option box:

   - **Paragraphs** .... [Alt] + [P]
     to convert each paragraph to a column marker.

   - **Tabs** .... [Alt] + [T]
     to convert each tab to a column marker.

   - **Commas** .... [Alt] + [M]
     to convert each comma to a column marker.

   - **Other** .... [Alt] + [O]
     to convert each instance of a character that you
     indicate to a column marker.

     Type character to convert to column marker ..... *character*

7. Click [**AutoFormat...**] .... [Alt] + [A]
   if desired, to apply AutoFormat to new
   table. *(See **TABLE AUTOFORMAT**, page 192.)*

8. Click [**OK**] .... [↵]

To convert table to text:

a. Position cursor in table to convert.

b. Click **Table, Select Table** .... [Alt] + [A] , [A]

c. Click **Table, Convert Table to Text**. [Alt] + [A] , [V]

*The **Convert Table to Text** dialog box displays.*

continued...

CONVERT TEXT TO TABLES (CONTINUED)

    d. Select one of the following column separator options:

- **Paragraphs**...................................... `Alt`+`P`
  to convert each cell to a separate paragraph.

- **Tabs**.. `Alt`+`T`
  to convert each column marker to a tab.

- **Commas**.. `Alt`+`M`
  to convert each column marker to a comma.

- **Other**.. `Alt`+`O`
  to convert each column marker to the
  character you indicate.

  Type character to convert column marker to ....*text*

    e. Click [**OK**] .... `↵`

Draw Table

1. Place cursor where you want to create table.

2. Click **Tables and Borders** button in **Standard** toolbar to display **Tables and Borders** toolbar, if necessary.

3. Click **Draw Table** button in **Tables and Borders** toolbar.

Pointer changes to:

4. Click and drag in document to create table outline, columns, and rows.

3. Click **Draw Table** button when finished.

Insert Table

INSERT TABLE USING MENU

*Inserts a table using the **Insert Table** command, allowing you to specify column widths and apply **AutoFormats**. This command also allows you to select the **Table Wizard**.*

1. Place cursor where you want to insert table.

2. Click T**a**ble, **I**nsert Table .... `Alt`+`A`,`I`

   *The **Insert Table** dialog box displays.*

3. Click **Number of _c_olumns** box ..... `Alt`+`C`, *number*
   and type desired number of
   columns (default is **2**).

4. Click **Number of _r_ows** box .... `Alt`+`R`, *number*
   and type number of rows (default is **2**).

5. Click **Column _w_idth** box .... `Alt`+`W`, *number*
   and type column width (default is **Auto**).

6. Click `AutoFormat...` .... `Alt`+`A`
   if you want to apply an **AutoFormat**
   to the table. *(See **TABLE AUTOFORMAT**, page 192.)*

7. Click `OK` ....`↵`

INSERT TABLE USING MOUSE

1. Place cursor where you want to insert table.

2. Click **Insert Table** button `⊞` in **Standard** toolbar.

3. Click and drag to select desired number
   of rows and columns from drop–down grid.

NAVIGATE IN TABLE

In addition to being able to point and click to move to different parts of a table, the following key combinations are available:

To Move to: Press:

Next Cell .... `Tab`

*If cursor is in last cell, pressing **Tab** adds another row.*

Previous Cell .... `Shift` + `Tab`

Right One Character .... `→`

Left One Character .... `←`

One Row Up .... `↑`

One Row Down .... `↓`

First Cell in Current Row .... `Alt` + `Home`

Last Cell in Current Row .... `Alt` + `End`

First Cell in Current Column .... `Alt` + `Page Up`

Last Cell in Current Column .... `Alt` + `Page Down`

Start New Paragraph .... `↵`

Add a New Row at Bottom of Table .... `Tab`

Cursor must be at end of last row.

SELECT INFORMATION IN A TABLE

*(See **SELECT INFORMATION**, page 33, for information on selecting in other parts of a document.)*

Select Cells

Click left mouse button in cell's selection bar (the unmarked area immediately left of text).

Select Rows

Click left mouse button in selection bar to left of row.

OR

1. Place cursor in row you want to select.

2. Click **Ta**ble, Select **R**ow .... Alt + A , R

Select Columns

1. Position mouse above column until it changes to: ↓

2. Click left mouse button.

    OR

    Hold **Alt** key .... Alt
    and click mouse in cell in column to select.

OR

1. Place cursor in column you want to select.

2. Click **Ta**ble, Select **C**olumn .... Alt + A , C

Select Entire Table

1. Place cursor in table you want to select.

2. Click **Ta**ble, Select T**a**ble .... Alt + A , A

    OR

    Press **Alt+NumPad 5** .... Alt + 5 *(NumPad)*

    Note: **Num Lock** *key must be turned on.*

SORT INFORMATION IN TABLE

1. Select information to sort (table
    rows or document paragraphs).

2. Click **Ta**ble, **S**ort .... Alt + A , S

*The **Sort** dialog box displays.*

continued...

190

3. Select first–tier sort options:

   a. Click **Sort by** box.................. `Alt`+`S`, `↑` `↓`
      and select first item by which
      to sort (column number, paragraph,
      field number, or name).

   b. Click **Type** box .... `Alt`+`Y`, `↑` `↓`
      and select how to sort information.

   c. Select sort direction from the following options:

   • **Ascending** .... `Alt`+`A`

   • **Descending** .... `Alt`+`D`

4. Select second–tier sort options:

   *Note: Some options may not be available
   depending on choices made in step 3.*

   a. Click **Then by** box .... `Alt`+`T`, `↑` `↓`
      and select second item by which to sort.

   b. Click **Type** box .... `Alt`+`P`, `↑` `↓`
      and select how to sort information.

   c. Select sort direction from the following options:

   • **Ascending** .... `Alt`+`C`

   • **Descending** .... `Alt`+`N`

5. Select third–tier sort options:

   *Note: Some options may not be available,
   depending on choices made in steps 3 & 4.*

   a. Click **Then by** box .... `Alt`+`B`, `↑` `↓`
      and select third item by which to sort.

   b. Click **Type** box .... `Alt`+`E`, `↑` `↓`
      and select how to sort information.

continued.

SORT INFORMATION IN TABLE (CONTINUED)

c. Select sort direction from the following options:

- **Ascending** .... `Alt` + `I`

- **Descending** .... `Alt` + `G`

6. Select one of the following **My List Has** options:

    *Note: This option is available only if a table was
    selected in step 1.*

- **Header row** .... `Alt` + `R`

- **No header row** .... `Alt` + `W`

To access additional sort options:

a. Click ▢ Options... ▢ .... `Alt` + `O`

*The **Sort Options** dialog box displays.*

b. Select character that separates each
   field in a record from the following:

    *Note: This option is only available if you are
    sorting document paragraphs, not tables.*

- **Tabs** .... `Alt` + `T`

- **Commas** .... `Alt` + `M`

- **Other** .... `Alt` + `O`
    Type other character .... *text*

c. Select from the following **Sort** options:

- **Sort column only** .... `Alt` + `R`
    to sort only selected column.

- **Case-sensitive** .... `Alt` + `C`
    to sort uppercase before lowercase words.

c. Click **Sorting language** .... `Alt` + `L`
   and select language to sort in.

7. Click ▢ **OK** ▢ .... `↵`

TABLE FORMATTING
Table AutoFormat

*Also see **AUTOFORMAT**, page 192.*

1. Place cursor in table to which you want to apply automatic formatting.

2. Click **T**able, Table Auto**F**ormat....... `Alt`+`A`,`F`

*The **Table AutoFormat** dialog box displays.*

3. Click **Forma**t**s** list box..............`Alt`+`T`,`↑``↓`
   and select desired format.

4. Select from the following **Formats to Apply** options:
   - **B**orders ....`Alt`+`B`
   - **S**hading..`Alt`+`S`
   - **F**ont ....`Alt`+`F`
   - **C**olor..`Alt`+`C`
   - AutoF**i**t ....`Alt`+`I`

5. Select from the following **Apply Special Formats To** options:
   - Heading **r**ows ....`Alt`+`R`
   - First c**o**lumn ....`Alt`+`O`
   - **L**ast row ....`Alt`+`L`
   - Last col**u**mn...`Alt`+`U`

6. Click [**OK**] .... `↵`

Adjust Column Width

ADJUST COLUMN WIDTH USING MENU

1. Select column(s) or cell(s) to change.

2. Double–click column marker in horizontal ruler.

   OR

   Click **Table**, **Cell Height and Width** ... `Alt`+`A`,`W`

   *The **Cell Height and Width** dialog box displays.*

3. Click `Column` .... `Alt`+`C`

4. Click **Width of Columns** box ..... `Alt`+`W`, *number* and type desired column width.

   *Notes: The name of **Width of Column** box changes to display numbers of selected columns (e.g., **Width of Columns 1–2**).*

   *To automatically adjust width of selected columns to fit the page margins, type **Auto**.*

   To change width of other columns:

   a. Click `Previous Column` .... `Alt`+`P`
      to select previous column.

      OR

      Click `Next Column` .... `Alt`+`N`
      to select next column.

   b. Repeat step 4 for each column to change.

   To automatically adjust width of selected columns according to their contents:

   Click `AutoFit` .... `Alt`+`A`

   *Note: Selecting this command closes the **Cell Height and Width** dialog box.*

continued...

ADJUST COLUMN WIDTH USING MENU (CONTINUED)

5. Click **Space Between Columns** ..... Alt + S , *number* box and type distance to place between columns.

6. Click [OK] .... ↵

ADJUST COLUMN WIDTH USING MOUSE

*Changes column width using mouse in Page Layout or Normal View (see **VIEW OPTIONS**, page 72).*

1. Select column to change.

2. Point at table column marker ▦ in horizontal ruler.

Mouse changes to: ↔

3. Click and drag marker to new position.

Whether you drag column gridlines or column markers in the ruler, the following procedures apply:

*   *Dragging the mouse by itself causes only selected columns or cells to resize.*

*   *Holding down **Shift** while dragging also adjusts table width.*

*   *Holding down **Shift+Ctrl** while dragging proportionally adjusts all columns and cells to right of selected columns or cells.*

*   *Holding **Ctrl** adjusts selected columns or cells immediately to the right of selected columns or cells.*

To automatically adjust width of selected columns or cells according to their contents:

a. Point at column gridline to right of selected columns/cells.

Mouse changes to: ◄‖►

b. Double–click left mouse button.

Adjust Row Height and Alignment

ADJUST ROW HEIGHT AND ALIGNMENT USING MENU

Changes the vertical height of rows and their horizontal alignment on a page. Also determines whether to allow page breaks to occur within a row.

1. Select row or column to change.

2. Double–click column marker on horizontal ruler ▦

   OR

   Click **T**a**b**le, Cell Height and **W**idth ... [Alt]+[A],[W]

   *The **Cell Height and Width** dialog box displays.*

3. Click [Row] .... [Alt]+[R]

4. Click **H**eight of Rows box.......... [Alt]+[E],[↑][↓]
   and select desired row height from list.

   *Notes: The name of the **Height of Rows** box
   changes to display the numbers of the
   selected rows (e.g., **Height of Rows 1–2**).*

   *To automatically adjust row height to fit
   the tallest entry, select **Auto**.*

   If you selected At Least or Exactly:

   Click **A**t box .... [Alt]+[A] , *number*
   and type desired row height.

5. Click **Indent** f**r**om Left box........ [Alt]+[F] , *number*
   if desired, and type distance to
   indent rows from the left page margin.

   To allow page breaks to occur within rows:

   Click **Allow row to** **b**reak across pages...... [Alt]+[B]
   check box.

continued...

ADJUST ROW HEIGHT & ALIGNMENT USING MENU (CONT)

6. Select one of the following options:

- **Left**... `Alt`+`L`

- **Center**... `Alt`+`T`

- **Right**... `Alt`+`I`

To change row height and alignment for other rows:

a. Click [**Previous Row**] .... `Alt`+`P`

OR

Click [**Next Row**] .... `Alt`+`N`

b. Repeats steps 4–6 to adjust additional rows.

7. Click [**OK**] .... `↵`

ADJUST ROW HEIGHT AND ALIGNMENT USING MOUSE

*Changes row heights using the mouse when in Page Layout View. (See **PAGE LAYOUT VIEW**, page 76.)*

1. Select row you want to change.

2. Place pointer on table row marker $|-|$ in vertical ruler to left of selected row.

Mouse changes to: ↕

3. Click and drag to new position, then release mouse button.

Insert Cells, Rows, and Columns
INSERT CELLS

1. Select a cell or group of cells.

> *Note:* *The number of new cells added will equal the number of cells selected.*

continued...

2. Click **Table, Insert Cells**.................. Alt + A , I

    OR

    Click **Insert Cells** button ⊟ in **Formatting** toolbar.

The **Insert Cells** *dialog box displays. This option is not available unless cell or group of cells is selected.*

3. Select how to insert new cells from the following:

    *   **Shift cells right**.................................. Alt + I

    *   **Shift cells down**.................................. Alt + D

    *   **Insert entire row**.............................. Alt + R

    *   **Insert entire column** .... Alt + C

4. Click [OK   ]...................................... ↵

INSERT ROWS

1. Select a row or group of rows.

    Notes: The number of new rows added will equal the number of rows selected.

    New rows are inserted above selected rows.

2. Click **Table, Insert Rows** .... Alt + A , I

    OR

    Click **Insert Rows** button ⊟ on **Formatting** toolbar.

    OR

    Place cursor outside last cell in row and press **Enter**....... ↵

A new row is inserted above the active row.

To insert new row at end of table:

Place cursor in last cell of last row and press **Tab**... Tab

INSERT COLUMNS

1. Select a column or group of columns.

    Notes: *The number of new columns added will equal the number of columns selected.*

    New columns are inserted to the left of the selected columns.

2. Click **Ta**ble, **I**nsert Columns .... `Alt`+`A`, `I`

    OR

    Click **Insert Columns** button ⬚ on **Formatting** toolbar.

    To insert new column to right of table:

    a. Place cursor in cell outside last column.

    b. Click **Ta**ble, **S**elect **C**olumn .... `Alt`+`A`, `C`

    c. Click **Ta**ble, **I**nsert Columns ...... `Alt`+`A`, `I`

Delete Cells, Rows, and Columns
DELETE CELLS

1. Select cell or group of cells to delete.

2. Click **Ta**ble, **D**elete Cells................ `Alt`+`A`, `D`

    *The **Delete Cells** dialog box displays.*

3. Select one of the following options:

    *   **Shift cells left** .... `Alt`+`L`
        to shift remaining cells in row to the left.

    *   **Shift cells up** .... `Alt`+`U`
        to shift remaining cells in column up.

    *   **Delete entire row** .... `Alt`+`R`

    *   **Delete entire column**........................ `Alt`+`C`

4. Click [OK] .... `↵`

DELETE ROWS OR COLUMNS

1. Select row(s) or column(s) to delete.
2. Click **Table**, **Delete Rows/Columns** ...... `Alt` + `A`, `D`

   OR

   Click **Edit**, **Cut** .... `Alt` + `E`, `T`

   OR

   Press **Ctrl+X** .... `Ctrl` + `X`

   OR

   Press **Shift+Delete** .... `Shift` + `Delete`

Merge Cells

Merges two or more adjacent cells into one cell. When cells are merged together, the contents of each are converted to paragraphs within the combined cell.

1. Select cells to merge.
2. Click **Table**, **Merge Cells** .... `Alt` + `A`, `M`

   OR

   Click **Merge Cells** button 🔲 in **Tables and Borders** toolbar.

Split Cells

1. Select cell or group of cells you want to split.
2. Click **Table**, **Split Cells** .... `Alt` + `A`, `P`

   OR

   Click **Split Cells** button 🔳 in the **Tables and Borders** toolbar.

*The **Split Cells** dialog box displays.*

3. Click **Number of columns** box .... `Alt` + `C`, *number* and type number of columns to split each cell into.

continued...

SPLIT CELLS (CONTINUED)

4. Click **Number of rows** box .... `Alt`+`R`, *number* and type number of rows to split each cell into.

5. Select or deselect **Merge cells before split.**

6. Click `OK` .... `↵`

Split Table

1. Place cursor in row to start a new table in.

2. Click **Table, Split Table** .... `Alt`+`A`, `T`

   OR

   Press **Shift+Ctrl+Enter** .... `Shift`+`Ctrl`+`↵`

   Note: Delete the paragraph mark between two tables to remove a split.

Insert Tabs in Cells

1. Place cursor in cell to insert a tab character in.

2. Press **Ctrl+Tab** .... `Ctrl`+`Tab`

   *Note: Word automatically aligns numbers and other information contained in a cell only if it is formatted with a single **decimal tab**.*

Insert Table Headings

Sets Word to recognize selected information as headings, which it will then automatically repeat and update on each page of a table spanning more than one page.

   Note: Table headings are not repeated or updated if a hard page break is inserted into table.

1. Select rows to designate as table headings.

2. Click **Table, Headings** .... `Alt`+`A`, `H`

Heading information is automatically copied and pasted into top rows of each page that table spans.

Display Gridlines

Notes: *Table gridlines that appear on screen do not print. If you want to print lines between table columns and rows, you need to add borders. (See **BORDERS AND SHADING**, page 90.)*

This command toggles display of gridlines for all tables within active document.

Click T**a**ble, Show **G**ridlines .... `Alt` + `A` , `G`
OR
Click T**a**ble, Hide **G**ridlines .... `Alt` + `A` , `G`

TABLE FORMULAS

Formulas are inserted in a table as fields that perform mathematical calculations using cell references. A reference refers to a cell's column letter and row number (e.g., A1, A2, B1, B2, etc.). Formulas consist of an equal sign (=), followed by a calculation function (SUM, AVERAGE, etc.), and parentheses containing the cell range to calculate, e.g., =SUM(A1:C5). Cells are referenced as follows:

Column Calculations *Cell ranges are referred to as ABOVE or BELOW the cursor, e.g., =SUM(ABOVE) adds all cells above cursor.*

Row Calculations *Cell ranges are referred to as LEFT or RIGHT of the cursor, e.g., =SUM(LEFT) adds all cells to left of cursor.*

Contiguous Ranges *Type starting and ending cells, separated by a colon, e.g., =SUM(A1:C5) adds all cells between A1 and C5.*

Noncontiguous Ranges *Type cell references, separated by commas, e.g., =SUM(A1,B2) adds cells A1 and B2.*

*The default calculation for a table is addition (SUM function). If you select the **Formula** command when your cursor is in a table, Word evaluates the location of the cursor and attempts to calculate the most logical cell range using the SUM function.*

continued...

202

TABLE FORMULAS (CONTINUED)

1. Place cursor in table where you want to insert formula.

2. Click **T**able, F**o**rmula .... Alt + A , O

*The **Formula** dialog box displays.*

3. Click **F**ormula box .... Alt + F , *text*
   and type formula and cell range.

   OR

   a. Click **Paste f**unction box...... Alt + U , ↑ ↓
      and select a function.

*Selected function is inserted after equal sign in **F**ormula box, and the cursor appears inside parentheses next to function.*

   b. Type cell range inside parentheses .....*cell range*

   To paste bookmark containing number reference in formula:

   a. Place cursor inside parentheses in **F**ormula box.

   b. Click **Paste b**ookmark box... Alt + B , ↑ ↓
      and select a bookmark.

   Note: The **Paste b**ookmark box is only available if you have a bookmark defined in your file.

4. Click **N**umber format box .... Alt + N , ↑ ↓
   and select a number format.

   Note: If the numbers being calculated include a number format (e.g., percentage), the formula result automatically appears in that format.

5. Click [OK] .... ↵

Results of formula appear in selected cell in table.

REFERENCES

BOOKMARKS

Bookmarks flag information in a document, making it easier to find. You can view bookmarks in a document by selecting the **View** *tab under* **Tools**, **Options**. (See **SCREEN DISPLAY OPTIONS**, page 78.)

Add a Bookmark

1. Select information or place cursor at location where you want to create bookmark.

2. Click **Insert, Bookmark**.................. `Alt` + `I`, `K`

   OR

   Press **Shift+Ctrl+F5**..................... `Shift` + `Ctrl` + `F5`

*The **Bookmark** dialog box displays.*

3. a. Click **Bookmark name** box .... `Alt` + `B`

   b. Type name for new bookmark .... *name*

      OR

      Select name of existing bookmark........ `↑` `↓`
      to redefine.

4. Click `    Add    ` .... `Alt` + `A`

   OR
   To delete bookmark:

   Click `    Delete    ` .... `Alt` + `D`

   Note: *You can also delete a bookmark by deleting the information associated with it.*

Go To Bookmark

> *Note:* You can also jump to a bookmark using the **Go To** command. (See **NAVIGATE**, page 25.)

1. Click **I**nsert, Boo**k**mark .... `Alt`+`I`, `K`

   OR

   Press **Shift+Ctrl+F5** .... `Shift`+`Ctrl`+`F5`

*The **Bookmark** dialog box displays.*

2. a. Click **B**ookmark name box ..... `Alt`+`B`, `↑` `↓`
      select bookmark to go to.

   b. Click [**Go To**] .... `Alt`+`G`

3. Click [**Close**] .... `Esc`

Show Bookmarks in Document

*See **SCREEN DISPLAY OPTIONS**, page 78.*

1. Click **T**ools, **O**ptions .... `Alt`+`T`, `O`

*The **Options** dialog box displays.*

2. Click [**View**]

3. Select **Book**marks check box.............. `Alt`+`K`

4. Click [**OK**] .... `↵`

CAPTIONS

*Numbered captions, created with **SEQ** fields, can be added to graphics, tables, and other information in a document. Numbered captions can be easily updated if a caption is moved, copied, or deleted. (See **FIELDS**, page 112, for information on updating and working with fields.)*

continued

1. Click item to add a caption to.

2. Click **I**nsert, **C**aption...................... `Alt`+`I`, `C`

*The **Caption** dialog box displays.*

3. Click **L**abel box .... `Alt`+`L`, `↑` `↓`
   and select appropriate label name
   (**Figure**, **Equation**, or **Table**).

   To create new label name:

   a. Click `New Label...` .... `Alt`+`N`

*The **New Label** dialog box displays.*

   b. Type new label..*label*

   c. Click `OK` .... `↵`

   To delete label name:

   a. Click **L**abel box .... `Alt`+`L`, `↑` `↓`
      and select label to delete.

   b. Click `Delete Label` .... `Alt`+`D`

   *Note: You cannot delete default labels
            (**Figure**, **Table**, **Equation**).*

4. Click **C**aption box .... `Alt`+`C`, *text*
   and type text for caption (defaults to
   label name selected in step 3, followed
   by a number).

   To change numbering format for captions:

   a. Click `Numbering...` .... `Alt`+`U`

*The **Caption Numbering** dialog box displays.*

   b. Click **F**ormat box............................... `F`, `↑` `↓`
      and select a numbering format.

continued..

CAPTIONS (CONTINUED)

To Include chapter number with caption number:

a. Select **Include chapter number** .... `C`

b. Click **Chapter starts with style** ..... `P`, `↑` `↓`
   and select style that chapter headings
   in your document are formatted with.

*Note: Once a chapter heading style is chosen,
          you cannot use it to format any other text
          in the document.*

c. Click **Use separator** .... `E`, `↑` `↓`
   and select a character to place between
   chapter heading and caption number.

d. Click `  OK  ` .... `↵`

5. Click **Position** box.................... `Alt`+`P`, `↑` `↓`
   and select a caption position
   (**Above Item** or **Below Item**).

   *Note: This option is only available if an item was
             selected in step 1.*

6. Click `  OK  ` .... `↵`

CROSS–REFERENCES

*Cross–references in Word, created with REF fields, refer to
footnotes, endnotes, bookmarks, captions, or paragraphs
created using heading styles. (See **FIELDS**, page 112, for more
information on updating and working with fields.)*

1. Place cursor where you want to insert cross–reference.

*Word suggests you type the text that begins the cross–
reference.(e.g., For more information, see . . .)*

2. Click **Insert**, **Cross–reference**......... `Alt`+`I`, `R`

continued..

*The **Cross–reference** dialog box displays.*

> *Note:* *The choices in the **Cross–reference** dialog box vary depending on the available reference items in the active document.*

3. Click **Reference type** box .... `Alt` + `T` , `↑` `↓`
   and select item to reference.

4. Click **Insert reference to** box .... `Alt` + `R` , `↑` `↓`
   and select type of information to display in cross–reference.

> *Notes:* *For example, you could select a chapter heading or page number. The cross–reference might read: "See also Getting Started" or "See also page 21." Word inserts the heading or page number, and automatically updates them after any changes.*

5. Select **Insert as hyperlink** .... `Alt` + `H`

> *Note:* *Selecting this option allows the reader to move directly from a cross–reference to the referenced item in the same document.*

6. Click **For which numbered item** ..... `Alt` + `W` , `↑` `↓`
   box and select item to refer to.

> *Note:* *Choices vary depending on selection in step 5.*

7. Click [**Insert**] .... `Alt` + `I`

8. Click [**Close**] .... `Esc`

FOOTNOTES/ENDNOTES
Insert Footnote or Endnote
INSERT FOOTNOTE OR ENDNOTE USING MENU

1. Place cursor where you want to insert footnote/endnote.

2. Click **I**nsert, Foot**n**ote .... `Alt`+`I`,`N`

*The **Footnote and Endnote** dialog box displays.*

3. Select type of note to insert from the following:

   • **F**ootnote.. `Alt`+`F`

   • **E**ndnote... `Alt`+`E`

4. Select type of numbering from the following:

   • **A**utoNumber .... `Alt`+`A`
     to automatically number notes, and update/
     renumber them when rearranged or edited.

   • **C**ustom Mark .... `Alt`+`C`
     to mark notes with character of your choice.

     Type character to use in place of numbers ....*text*

   To insert special character from Symbol dialog box:

   Click `Symbol...` .... `Alt`+`S`
   and follow steps 4–5 in **Insert Symbols**, page 107.

5. Click `OK` .... `↵`

*The **Note** pane displays in document.*

6. Type footnote or endnote text............................ *text*

7. Click anywhere in document to continue.

1. Place cursor where you want to insert footnote/endnote.

2. Press **Ctrl+Alt+F**.......................... Ctrl + Alt + F
    to insert footnote.
    *The **Footnote** pane dialog box displays.*

    OR

    Press **Ctrl+Alt+E**.......................... Ctrl + Alt + E
    to insert endnote.

*The **Endnote** pane displays at the end of the document.*

> Note: If last footnote or endnote inserted in
> document used **AutoNumber** format, the next
> consecutive **AutoNumber** footnote or endnote
> is inserted. If last footnote or endnote inserted
> in document used a custom mark, **Footnote
> and Endnote** dialog box displays.

3. Type footnote or endnote text........................... *text*
4. Click anywhere in document to continue.

Display Footnote/Endnote

*Displays the **Note** pane and allows you to view footnotes and
endnotes in a document. You can also display footnotes and
endnotes when in **Print Preview** or **Page Layout View**.*

> Note: You can jump to a footnote or endnote
> using the **Go To** command. (See
> **NAVIGATE**, page 25.)

Double–click footnote or endnote mark in document at
the bottom of the screen.

OR

1. Click **T**ools, **O**ptions .... Alt + T , O

*The **Options** dialog box displays.*

2. Click [View]

continued...

210

DISPLAY FOOTNOTE/ENDNOTE (CONTINUED)

3. Select **Screen Tips** check box under **Show** .. `Alt`+`R`

4. Click `OK` .... `⏎`

5. Rest pointer on note reference mark in document.

*The **note reference mark** is the number that appears to the left of the referenced point in the document. When the pointer rests on the reference mark, the note text appears above it.*

Edit Footnote/Endnote

1. Double–click **reference mark** in document for footnote/endnote to edit. *(See **Display Footnote/Endnote**, page 209.)*

*The **Note** pane displays.*

2. Make desired changes to footnotes or endnotes.

Delete a Footnote/Endnote

1. Select the **reference mark** for the footnote or endnote you want to delete.

2. Press **Delete** .... `Delete`

   OR

   Press **Backspace** .... `Backspace`

Edit All Footnotes

1. Click **I**nsert, Foot**n**ote .... `Alt`+`I`, `N`

*The **Footnote and Endnote** dialog box displays.*

2. Click `Options...` .... `Alt`+`O`

*The **Note Options** dialog box displays.*

3. Click `All Footnotes` .... `Alt`+`F`

continued.

211

EDIT ALL FOOTNOTES (CONTINUED)

4. Click **P**lace at box .... Alt + P , ↑ ↓
   and select where to place footnotes
   (**Bottom of Page** or **Beneath Text**).

5. Click **N**umber format box .... Alt + N , ↑ ↓
   and select a footnote number format.

6. Click **Start at** box.................... Alt + A , *number*
   and type starting number for footnotes.

7. Select **Numbering** sequence from the following:

   • **C**ontinuous .... Alt + C

   • **Restart Each S**ection .... Alt + S

   • **Restart Each Pa**ge .... Alt + G

8. Click [OK] .... ↵

Edit All Endnotes

1. Click **I**nsert, Foot**n**ote.................... Alt + I , N

*The **Footnote and Endnote** dialog box displays.*

2. Click [**O**ptions...] .... Alt + O

*The **Note Options** dialog box displays.*

3. Click [All **E**ndnotes] .... Alt + E

4. Click **P**lace at box .... Alt + P , ↑ ↓
   and select where to place endnotes
   (**End of Section** or **End of Document**).

5. Click **N**umber format box .... Alt + N , ↑ ↓
   and select number format for endnotes.

continued...

EDIT ALL ENDNOTES (CONTINUED)

6. Click **Start At** box...................... `Alt`+`A`, *number*
   and type starting number for endnotes.

7. Select **Numbering** sequence from the following:

   - **Continuous**... `Alt`+`C`

   - **Restart Each Section**........................ `Alt`+`S`

8. Click `OK` .... `↵`

Convert Footnotes to Endnotes and Endnotes to Footnotes

1. Click **Insert, Footnote** .... `Alt`+`I`, `N`

*The **Footnote and Endnote** dialog box displays.*

2. Click `Options...` ....`Alt`+`O`

   *Note: This option is only available if footnotes or
   endnotes have been inserted in document.*

*The **Note Options** dialog box displays.*

3. Click `Convert...` ....`Alt`+`T`

*The **Convert Notes** dialog box displays.*

4. Select one of the following options:

   - **Convert all footnotes to endnotes**....... `Alt`+`F`

   - **Convert all endnotes to footnotes**....... `Alt`+`E`

   - **Swap footnotes and endnotes**............. `Alt`+`S`

5. Click `OK` .... `↵`

INDEX AND TABLES

Indexes and tables in Word 97 are created using fields. (See **FIELDS***, page 112, for information on working with fields.*

Index
MARK INDEX ENTRY

Marks index entries for compilation into an index.

1. Select information to use as index entry, or position cursor where you want to insert index entry.

   Note: *To refer to multiple pages in an entry, mark all text to refer to with a bookmark. (See* ***Add Bookmark****, page 112.)*

2. a. Click **Insert, Index and Tables ..** `Alt` + `I`, `D`

   The **Index and Tables** *dialog box displays.*

   b. Click `Index` .... `Alt` + `X`

   c. Click `Mark Entry...` .... `Alt` + `K`

   OR

   Press **Shift+Alt+X** .... `Shift` + `Alt` + `X`

   The **Mark Index Entry** *dialog box displays.*

3. Click **Main entry** box .... `Alt` + `E`, *text*
   and type or edit index entry text.

   Note: *Any text selected in step 1 automatically appears in the* **Main entry** *box.*

4. Click **Subentry** box, if desired......... `Alt` + `S`, *text*
   and type subentry text.

   Note: *To include a third–level entry, type the subentry text followed by a colon and the third–level text.*

continued...

214

5. Select one of the following reference options:

- **Cross–reference**............................... `Alt`+`C`
  to list cross–reference text, rather than
  a page number, in the index entry.

  Type cross–reference text ....*text*

  Note: *You can format cross–reference text using*
  *shortcut keys. (See **CHARACTER***
  ***FORMATTING**, page 101.)*

- **Current page**..................................... `Alt`+`P`
  to list current page number in index entry.

- **Page range**...................................... `Alt`+`R`
  to list a page range in the index entry.

  Note: *To use this option, you must first mark the*
  page range to refer to with a bookmark.
  Then select the bookmark name from
  *drop–down box under **Page range** option.*

6. Select one of the following **Page number formats**:

- **Bold** .... `Alt`+`B`

- **Italic** .... `Alt`+`I`

7. Click [**Mark**] .... `Alt`+`M`

   OR

   Click [**Mark All**] .... `Alt`+`A`

   Note: ***Mark All** is only available if text was selected*
   in step 1. This option marks first occurrence in
   each paragraph that exactly matches
   uppercase and lowercase letters in entry.

8. Click the **Show/Hide** ¶ button, if desired, on the
   Standard toolbar to display or hide index markings.

9. Click [**Close**] .... `Esc`

COMPILE INDEX

Creates index based on marked entries in document.

1. Place cursor where you want to insert index.

2. Click **I**nsert, In**d**ex and Tables .... `Alt`+`I`,`D`

*The **Index and Tables** dialog box displays.*

3. Click [Inde**x**] .... `Alt`+`X`

4. Select index type from the following options:

   • In**d**ented .... `Alt`+`D`

   • Ru**n**–in .... `Alt`+`N`

5. Click **Forma**t**s** list box.............. `Alt`+`T`,`↑``↓`
   and select desired index format.

   OR

   To create custom index format:

   a. Click **Forma**t**s** list box.......... `Alt`+`T`,`↑``↓`
      and select **From Template**.

   b. Click [**M**odify...] .... `Alt`+`M`

*The **Style** dialog box displays.*

   c. Follow steps 2–4 in **Modify Style**, page 146.

6. Select **H**eading for accented letters ...... `Alt`+`H`
   check box, if desired, to sort words
   beginning with an accented letter
   under a separate heading.

7. Select **R**ight align page numbers .... `Alt`+`R`
   check box, if desired.

   Note: This option is unavailable if
   ***Run–in** was selected in step 4.*

continued..

COMPILE INDEX (CONTINUED)

8. Click **Co̲lumns** box................... `Alt`+`O`, *number*
and type desired number of index
columns per page.

9. Click **Ta̲b Leader** box............... `Alt`+`B`,`↑``↓`
if desired, and select a tab leader
(ellipses, dashes, or a solid line) to
place between each index entry and its
corresponding page number. *(See **Set
Tab Stops**, page 157.)*

> Note: *This option is only available if **Indented**
> was selected in step 4, and **Right align
> page numbers** was selected in step 7.*

10. Click [OK   ] .... `↵`

Table of Contents
MARK TABLE OF CONTENTS ENTRY

*Marks table of contents entries for compilation into a
table of contents. To create table of contents, apply
heading styles to headings you want to include in
the table (see **STYLES**, page 146, for more information).
You can also use styles that include **outline–level**
formats. (See **Format Multilevel List**, page 97.)*

1. Select information to use as table entry, or position
cursor where you want to insert table entry.

2. Press **Shift+Alt+O** .... `Shift`+`Alt`+`O`

*The **Mark Table of Contents Entry** dialog box displays.*

3. Click **E̲ntry** box............................. `Alt`+`E`, *text*
and type table entry text.

continued

MARK TABLE OF CONTENTS ENTRY (CONTINUED)

*Note: Any text selected in step 1 automatically
appears in the __Entry__ box by default.*

4. Click **Table identifier** box......... `Alt`+`I`, `↑` `↓`
    if document has more than one table
    of contents, and then select letter for
    table of contents to add entry to.

5. Click **Level** box...................... `Alt`+`L`, *number*
    and type desired entry level.

6. Click | __M__ark | .... `Alt`+`M`

COMPILE TABLE OF CONTENTS

*Compiles table of contents in current document. By default,
Word compiles table of contents from heading styles, although
you can also use other styles and table entry fields.*

1. Place cursor where you want to insert table of contents.

2. Click **Insert, Index and Tables** .... `Alt`+`I`, `D`

*The **Index and Tables** dialog box displays.*

3. Click | Table of Contents | .... `Alt`+`C`

4. Click **Formats** list box.............. `Alt`+`T`, `↑` `↓`
    and select a table of contents format.

    OR

    To create a custom table of contents format:

    a. Click **Formats** box .... `Alt`+`T`, `↑` `↓`
        and select **From Template**.

    b. Click | __M__odify... | .... `Alt`+`M`

*The **Style** dialog box displays.*

    c. Follow steps 2–4 in **Modify Style**, page 150.

continued...

218

COMPILE TABLE OF CONTENTS (CONTINUED)

5. Select from the following page number options:

   - **S**how Page Numbers .... `Alt`+`S`

   - **R**ight Align Page Numbers .... `Alt`+`R`

6. Click **Show levels** box .... `Alt`+`L`, *number*
   and type number of entry levels to
   list in table of contents.

7. Click **Tab leader** box................. `Alt`+`B`, `↑` `↓`
   if desired, and select tab leader
   (ellipses, dashes, or a solid line) to
   place between each table of contents
   entry and its corresponding page
   number. *(See **Set Tab Stops**, page 157.)*

   *Note: This option is only available if **Right align
   page numbers** was selected in step 5.*

**To create table of contents with styles
other than standard heading styles, or
to include table entry fields:**

   *Note: Skip this step if you have used standard
   heading and caption styles in document,
   and want Word to automatically locate
   those styles and use them to create table.*

   a. Click [**Options...**] .... `Alt`+`O`

*The **Table of Contents Options** dialog box displays.*

   b. Click **TOC level** .... `Alt`+`L`, *number*
      and, in the boxes across from each
      heading style, type a corresponding
      table of contents level. (Styles selected
      for use in compiling the table of contents
      have check marks next to them.)

continued.

219

COMPILE TABLE OF CONTENTS (CONTINUED)

c. Select **Table entry fields** .... `Alt`+`E`
   check box, if desired, to include table
   entry fields when compiling table of contents.

d. Deselect **Styles** check box .... `Alt`+`S`
   if desired, to use only table entry fields
   when compiling table of contents.

e. Click [**Reset**] .... `Alt`+`R`
   if desired, to restore default TOC
   settings (heading styles 1–3 are used
   as table of contents levels 1–3).

f. Click [**OK**] .... `↵`
   to close **Table of Contents Options** dialog box.

8. Click [**OK**] .... `↵`

Table of Figures
CREATE TABLE OF FIGURES

Compiles a table of figures from captions (default), or from styles and table entry fields.

> Note: To create table of figures, you must first label figures in document with captions. (See **CAPTIONS**, page 204.) If you have already labeled your figures, you can apply a custom style to identify their labels as captions, so they can be used to build table of figures.

1. Place cursor where you want to insert table of figures.

2. Click **Insert**, **Index and Tables** .... `Alt`+`I`, `D`

*The **Index and Tables** dialog box displays.*

3. Click [Table of Figures] .... `Alt`+`F`

220

4. Click **Caption label** list box.......`Alt`+`L`,`↑``↓`
   and select caption label to use when
   compiling table of figures.

   OR

   **To create table of figures from a custom style, or
   to include table entry fields:**

   a. Click ▐ **Options...** ▌ ....`Alt`+`O`

   *The **Table of Figures Options** dialog box displays.*

   b. Click **Style** check box...........`Alt`+`S`,`↑``↓`
      and then click box to the right of
      it and select style to create table
      of figures from.

   Note: *All figure captions to be included in table of
             figures must be formatted in same custom
             style, and that style must be applied only
             to captions.*

   c. Click **Table entry fields** ....`Alt`+`E`
      if desired, to base table of figures on
      table entry fields, instead of, or in
      addition to, styles.

   d. Click **Table Identifier** box....`Alt`+`I`,`↑``↓`
      and select a letter to identify the table
      entry fields to include in table of figures.

   e. Click ▐ **OK** ▌ ....`↵`

5. Click **Formats** list box...............`Alt`+`T`,`↑``↓`
   and select a table of figures format.

   OR

continued.

CREATE TABLE OF FIGURES (CONTINUED)

To create custom table of figures format:

a. Click **Formats** list box.......... `Alt`+`T`, `↑` `↓`
   and select **From Template**.

b. Click [**Modify...**] .... `Alt`+`M`

*The **Style** dialog box displays.*

c. Follow steps 2–4 in **Modify Style**, page 150.

6. Select from the following page number options:

   • **Show page numbers** .... `Alt`+`S`

   • **Right align page numbers** .... `Alt`+`R`

   • **Include label and number**................... `Alt`+`N`

7. Click **Tab Leader** box .... `Alt`+`B`, `↑` `↓`
   if desired, and select tab leader
   (ellipses, dashes, or a solid line) to
   place between each table of figures
   entry and its corresponding page number.
   *(See **Set Tab Stops**, page 157.)*

   *Note: This option is only available if **Right align
   page numbers** was selected in step 6.*

8. Click [**OK**] .... `↵`

Table of Authorities

*Note: To create table of authorities, you must
first mark all citations in document.*

*Tables of Authorities are created using long citations and short
citations. Long citations in a legal document are used only
once and contain the entire text of the citation. All further
references to the same source are short citations containing a
summary of the corresponding long citation.*

MARK CITATIONS

1. Select information to use as a long citation, or position cursor where you want to insert a citation entry.

2. a. Click **Insert**, **Index and Tables** .... `Alt`+`I`,`D`

*The **Index and Tables** dialog box displays.*

    b. Click [Table of Authorities] .... `Alt`+`A`

    c. Click [**Mark Citation...**] .... `Alt`+`K`

    OR

    Press **Shift+Alt+I** .... `Shift`+`Alt`+`I`

*The **Mark Citation** dialog box displays.*

> *Notes:* *Any text selected in step 1 automatically appears in **Selected Text** and **Short Citation** boxes.*
>
> *You can format citation entries in **Mark Citations** dialog box using shortcut keys. (See **CHARACTER FORMATTING**, page 101.)*

3. Click **Selected text** box................. `Alt`+`T`, *text* and create or edit long citation text for Word to search for when compiling table of authorities.

4. Click **Category** box.................... `Alt`+`C`, `↑` `↓` and select a citation category.

    To modify citation category:

    a. Click [**Category...**] .... `Alt`+`G`

*The **Edit Category** dialog box displays.*

    b. Click **Category** list box........ `Alt`+`C`, `↑` `↓` and select citation category to modify.

continued

   c. Click **Replace <u>w</u>ith** box .... `Alt`+`W`, *text*
     and type replacement text for
     citation category.

   d. Click ` Replace ` .... `Alt`+`R`

   e. Click ` OK ` .... `↵`
     to close **Edit Category** dialog box.

5. Click **<u>S</u>hort Citation** box .... `Alt`+`S`
   and create or edit short citation text for
   Word to search for when compiling
   table of authorities.

6. Click ` Mark ` .... `Alt`+`M`
   to mark single occurrence of citation.
   OR
   Click ` Mark All ` .... `Alt`+`A`
   to mark all occurrences of short and long citations.

   To mark additional citations in the document:

   a. Click ` Next Citation ` .... `Alt`+`N`

   b. Repeat steps 3–6 for each additional citation.

7. Click ` Close ` .... `Esc`

COMPILE TABLE OF AUTHORITIES

1. Mark citations in document. *(See **Mark Citations**, above)*.

2. Place cursor where you want to insert table
   of authorities.

continued. .

224

3. Click **Insert**, **Index and Tables**........ `Alt` + `I` , `D`

   *The **Index and Tables** dialog box displays.*

4. Click [Table of Authorities] .... `Alt` + `A`

5. Click **Formats** list box.............. `Alt` + `T` , `↑` `↓`
   and select a table of authorities format.

   OR

   To create custom table of authorities format:

   a. Click **Formats** box.............. `Alt` + `T` , `↑` `↓`
      and select **From Template.**

   b. Click [Modify...] .... `Alt` + `M`

   *The **Style** dialog box displays*

   c. Follow steps 2–4 in **Modify Style**, page 150.

6. Select from the following format options:

   • **Use passim** .... `Alt` + `P`

   • **Keep original formatting**.................... `Alt` + `R`

7. Click **Category** box..................... `Alt` + `G` , `↑` `↓`
   and select category to compile citations for.

8. Click **Tab Leader** box............... `Alt` + `B` , `↑` `↓`
   if desired, and select tab leader
   (ellipses, dashes, or a solid line) to
   place between each table of authorities
   entry and its corresponding page
   number.*(See **Set Tab Stops**, page 157.)*

9. Click [OK] .... `↵`

Update Tables

When you have edited a document so that page numbers or text included in a table have changed, update the table.

1. Click anywhere in table to select it.

   Note: Indexes and Tables of Contents, Figures and Authorities are all fields. Selecting a field selects the entire table.

2. Press **F9** .... `F9`

PROOFING AND REVIEW TOOLS
AUTOCORRECT

Automatically corrects common errors as you type, such as misspellings, incorrect capitalization, and other text that you specify.

1. Place your cursor anywhere in document, or select text to replace.

2. Click **Tools**, **AutoCorrect** .... `Alt`+`T`,`A`

*The **AutoCorrect** dialog box displays.*

3. Select from the following **AutoCorrect** options:

   - **Correct TWo INitial CApitals** .... `Alt`+`O`
   - **Capitalize first letter of sentences** .... `Alt`+`S`
   - **Capitalize names of days** .... `Alt`+`N`
   - **Correct accidental usage** .... `Alt`+`L`
     of cAPS LOCK Key
   - **Replace text as you type** .... `Alt`+`T`

   To add new AutoCorrect entry:

   a. Click **Replace** box .... `Alt`+`R`, *text*
      and type text you want automatically replaced as you type.

continued..

AUTOCORRECT (CONTINUED)

b. Click <u>With</u> box .... `Alt`+`W`, *text*
and type text to replace text
typed in step a with.

*Note: Any text selected in step 1 automatically
appears in the **With** dialog box.*

c. Click <u>P</u>lain .... `Alt`+`P`
to not store formatting with the entry
if you selected text in step 1.

OR

Click <u>F</u>ormatted .... `Alt`+`F`
to store formatting with the entry if
you selected text in step 1.

d. Click [<u>A</u>dd] .... `Alt`+`A`

To delete existing AutoText entry:

a. Select **AutoText** entry........................... `↑` `↓`
to delete from list box in **AutoCorrect** window.

b. Click [<u>D</u>elete] .... `Alt`+`D`

To change existing AutoText entry:

a. Select **AutoText** entry........................... `↑` `↓`
to change from list box in **AutoCorrect** window.

b. Click <u>With</u> box .... `Alt`+`W`, *text*
and type text with which to replace
AutoText entry selected in step a.

c. Click [Rep<u>l</u>ace] .... `Alt`+`A`

4. Click [OK] .... `↵`

COMMENTS

*Use comments to annotate your documents or to add reviewer's comments. You can have others review a document by giving them a copy and having them type comments. Reviewers' comments appear in a document as hidden text, and are marked with color–coded initials. By default, Word uses the user name and initials entered in the **User Information** tab of the **Options** dialog box. See **USER INFORMATION**, page 37, for information on changing reviewer name and initials.*

*Comments can be printed with the document or by themselves. (See **PRINT**, page 29.)*

Insert Comments

1. Place cursor where you want to insert comment.

2. Click **I**nsert, Co**m**ment .... Alt + I , M

   OR

   Press **Ctrl+Alt+M**......................... Ctrl + Alt + M

   OR

   Click **Insert Comment** button in **Reviewing** toolbar. *(See **TOOLBARS**, page 82.)*

*A comment or reviewer mark, consisting of the reviewer's initials and a number, is inserted, and the **Comments** pane displays.*

3. Type comment text... *text*

4. Click Close .... Shift + Alt + C
   to close **Comments** pane.

Display Comments

> *Note:* *You can jump to a comment using the* ***Go To*** *command. (See* ***NAVIGATE***, *page 25, for more information.)*

Rest pointer on top of yellow shaded text.

Reviewer name and comment displays.

> *Note:* *If comments do not display, you need to select* ***Screen Tips*** *on the* ***View*** *tab under* ***Tools***, ***Options***. *See* ***SCREEN DISPLAY OPTIONS***, *page 78.*

OR

1. Click **View**, **Comments** .... `Alt`+`V`,`C`

The ***Comments*** *pane displays.*

2. Click **Comments From** box......... `Alt`+`R`,`↑``↓`
   and select reviewer comments
   to display(default is **All Reviewers**).

3. Click `Close` .... `Shift`+`Alt`+`C`
   to close **Comments** pane.

Delete Comment

1. Select comment mark in document to delete.

2. Click **Delete Comment** button [✖] in **Reviewer** toolbar. *(See* ***TOOLBARS***, *page 82.)*

GRAMMAR CHECK

See ***Spell and Grammar Check***, *page 238.*

HIGHLIGHTER PEN

Marks selected text for emphasis or to note revisions.

1. Click **Highlight** icon 🖉 ▾ on **Formatting** toolbar.

2. Select information to highlight.

   To select a different highlighting color:

   a. Click drop–down arrow next to **Highlight** icon 🖉 ▾

   Note: *To remove highlighting, select highlighted text and click **Highlight** icon.*

   b. Select new color .... ⬆ ⬇ ➡ ⬅ , ⏎

3. Click **Highlight** icon again or press **Esc** .... Esc
   to turn off highlighting.

HYPHENATION

1. Click **T**ools, **L**anguage .... Alt + T , L

2. Click **H**yphenation .... H

*The **Hyphenation** dialog box displays.*

3. Select from the following hyphenation options:

   • **A**utomatically Hyphenate Document .... Alt + A

   • Hyphenate Words in **C**APS .... Alt + C

4. Click **Hyphenation z**one box ..... Alt + Z , *number*
   and type desired distance from
   right margin in which to hyphenate
   words (default is **0.25"**).

5. Click **L**imit Consecutive .... Alt + L , *number*
   Hyphens To box and type maximum
   number of lines that can end in
   hyphens (default is **No Limit**).

continued...

HYPHENATION (CONTINUED)

To hyphenate a document manually:

a. Click [**Manual...**] .... [Alt] + [M]

The ***Manual Hyphenation*** *dialog box displays.*

b. Click mouse to change hyphen position.

c. Click [**Yes**] .... [Alt] + [Y]
   to hyphenate word at selected position.

OR

Click [**No**] .... [Alt] + [N]
to skip current word and move to
next word to be hyphenated.

6. Click [**OK**] .... [↵]

LANGUAGE

Changes language setting for selected information, so that Word proofing tools check it according to rules of selected language. Also sets the default language for the active template. (See ***SPELL AND GRAMMAR CHECK****, page 238, for more information. Also see your Word documentation for information on obtaining additional language dictionaries.)*

1. Select text to format in a different language.

2. Click **Tools**, **Language** .... [Alt] + [T], [L]

3. Click **Set Language** .... [Alt] + [L], [↑][↓]
   and select a language from submenu.

Word will check only the selected text in the language you have specified.

continued.

To change default language for active template:

a. Click [**Default...**] .... Alt + D

b. Click [**Yes**] .... Alt + Y
   when confirmation dialog box appears.

4. Click [**OK**] .... ↵

PROTECT DOCUMENT

You can protect Word documents so that reviewers can make comments, but not revisions; or so that reviewers can make marked revisions only; or so that users can fill in form fields, but cannot otherwise alter the file. (See **COMMENTS***, page 227, and* **FORMS***, page 42. Also see* **Save Options***, page 56, for information on assigning a password to prevent a document from being opened.)*

1. Click **Tools**, **Protect Document**....... Alt + T , P

The **Protect Document** *dialog box displays.*

2. Select one of the following **Protect document for** options:

   • **Tracked changes** .... Alt + T
     to allow reviewers to make highlighted
     changes, which the author can track.

   • **Comments**..................................... Alt + C
     to allow reviewers to insert comments,
     but not to change the document.

   • **Forms** .... Alt + F
     to allow changes only in forms or
     unprotected sections.

continued...

232

PROTECT DOCUMENT (CONTINUED)

To protect specific sections of a form:

a. Click `Sections...` .... `Alt` + `S`

Note: This option is only available if the document contains more than one section.

*The **Section Protection** dialog box displays.*

b. Click **P**rotected sections... `Alt` + `P` , `↑` , `↓` , `Space` box and select sections to protect.

c. Click `OK` .... `↵`
to close **Section Protection** dialog box.

*The **Protect Document** dialog box redisplays.*

To assign optional password:

Click **P**assword box .... `Alt` + `P` , *password* and type desired password.

3. Click `OK` .... `↵`

Unprotect Document

1. Click **T**ools, **U**nprotect Document ...... `Alt` + `T` , `P`

*Note: If a password was selected with the **Protect Document** command, the **Unprotect Document** dialog box displays, prompting you for the selected password.*

2. Type password, if necessary.................. *password*

3. Click `OK` .... `↵`

Protect Form

*Toggles form protection for active document. (Does not affect protection of form fields. See **PROTECT DOCUMENT**, page 231, for information on password protecting a form, or specific sections of a form.)*

Click **Protect Form** button 🔒 on **Forms** toolbar. *(See **TOOLBARS**, page 82.)*

REVISION MARKS

*Marks revisions to document, so you can track changes, as well as differentiate between different reviewers' changes. You can accept or reject any marked change. How revision marks are displayed in a document is selected in the **Track Changes** tab under **Tools**, **Options**. (See **Revision Marker Options**, page 234.)*

Turn Revisions On and Off

> Note: When revision marks are turned on, the **TRK** message in the status bar is bold.

1. Double–click **TRK** message ⌷TRK⌷ in status bar.

   OR

   a. Click **Tools**, **Track changes** .... [Alt]+[T], [T]

   b. Click **Highlight Changes** .... [H]

*The **Highlight Changes** dialog box displays.*

2. Select **Track changes while editing** .... [Alt]+[T] check box.

3. Select from the following options:

   - **Highlight changes on screen** .... [Alt]+[S] to display marks on screen as you edit.

   - **Highlight changes in printed document** .... [Alt]+[P] to display marks in printed document.

continued...

234

TURN REVISIONS ON AND OFF (CONTINUED)

To hide revision marks:

Deselect **Highlight changes on screen** and **Highlight changes in printed document**.

OR

Double–click **TRK** message `TRK` in status bar.

To select how revision marks are displayed in document:

Click `Options...` .... `Alt` + `O`
*(See **Revision Marker Options**, below.)*

4. Click `OK` .... `↵`

Revision Marker Options

1. Click **Tools**, **Options** .... `Alt` + `T` , `O`

*The **Options** dialog box displays.*

2. Click `Track Changes`

3. Select desired **Inserted Text** options:

   a. Click **Mark** box .... `Alt` + `M` , `↑` `↓`
   and select a format to use to mark new text inserted during review.

   b. Click **Color** box .... `Alt` + `C` , `↑` `↓`
   and select color to use to mark new text inserted during review.

   Note: *For this and all following color choices, selecting **By Author** assigns a unique color to each of the first eight revisers. Clicking **Auto** marks all revisions with default color. Clicking a single color marks revisions by all reviewers with same color.*

continued.

4. Select **Deleted Text** options:

    a. Click **Mark** box .... `Alt`+`A`, `↑``↓`
        and select format to use to mark
        text deleted during review.

    b. Click **Color** box .... `Alt`+`O`, `↑``↓`
        and select a color to use to
        mark text deleted during review.

5. Select desired **Changed Formatting** options:

    a. Click **Mark** box .... `Alt`+`R`, `↑``↓`
        and select a format to use to
        mark lines containing revised text.

    b. Click **Color** box .... `Alt`+`L`, `↑``↓`
        and select a color to use to mark
        lines containing revised text.

6. Select **Changed Lines** options:

    a. Click **Mark** box .... `Alt`+`K`, `↑``↓`
        and select a line style for
        markers (vertical bars) in
        margins next to lines
        containing revised text.

    b. Click **Color** box .... `Alt`+`R`, `↑``↓`
        and select a color for markers
        (vertical bars) in margins next
        to lines containing revised text.

7. Click [**OK**] .... `↵`

236

Review and Accept/Reject Revisions

REVIEW AND ACCEPT/REJECT REVISIONS USING MENU

1. Double–click **TRK** message `TRK` in status bar.

2. Place cursor where you want to start review.

3. Click **Tools**, **Track Changes** .... `Alt` + `T` , `T`

4. Click **Accept or Reject Changes** .... `A`

*The **Accept or Reject Changes** dialog box displays.*

To accept/reject individual changes:

a. Click `⇨ Find` or `⬅ Find` .... `F` or `I`
   to select change to review.

b. Click `Accept` or `Reject` .... `A` or `R`

To accept/reject all changes:

a. Click `Accept All` or `Reject All` ...... `C` or `J`

b. Click `Yes` ....`Alt` + `Y`
   when confirmation dialog box appears.

5. Click `Close` to exit the **Accept or Reject** dialog box.

REVIEW AND ACCEPT/REJECT REVISIONS USING MOUSE

1. Display **Reviewing** toolbar. *(See TOOLBARS, page 82.)*

2. Click **Next Change** 📑 in **Reviewing** toolbar.
   OR
   Click **Previous Change** 📑 in **Reviewing** toolbar.

continued..

REVIEW & ACCEPT/REJECT REVISIONS USING MOUSE (CONT)

3. Click **Accept Change** 🖮 to keep the change and remove revision marks.

   OR

   Click **Reject Change** 🖮 to undo the change and remove revision marks.

4. Repeat steps 2–3 to review changes as desired.

Compare Versions

Compares two versions of a document, inserting revision marks where a revised document differs from the original.

1. Open revised version of document.

2. Click **T̲ools, T̲rack Changes**............ `Alt`+`T`,`T`

3. Click **C̲ompare Documents** .... `C`

*The **Select Files to Compare Current Document** dialog box displays.*

4. Click **Files of T̲ype** box............. `Alt`+`T`,`↑``↓`
   and select type of file to compare
   with the current document.

5. Open file to compare with current document. *(See OPEN FILE, page 52.)*

Word compares documents and marks changes in current one.

6. Accept or reject marked revisions in current document. *(See **Review and Accept/Reject Revisions**, page 236.)*

   Note: *If revised document contains revision marks, a prompt displays, informing you that Word may not be able to detect some revisions. Remove revision marks with procedures in **Review and Accept/Reject Revisions**, page 236.*

Merge Revised Documents

Merges revisions/comments from revised document into original.

1. Open document in which to display merged revision marks/comments from all documents.

2. Double–click **MRK** message ⬛MRK⬛ in status bar.
   OR
   Click **Tools, Merge Documents** ...... ⬛Alt⬛ + ⬛T⬛,⬛D⬛

*The **Select Files to Merge into Current Document** dialog box displays.*

3. Click **File name** box .... ⬛Alt⬛ + ⬛N⬛, *filename* and type name of file to merge.
   OR
   Double–click document containing revisions/comments to merge.

4. Repeat steps 2–3 for each additional document.

SPELL AND GRAMMAR CHECK

Note: *Various spelling/grammar check options can be selected in **Spelling and Grammar** tab under **Tools, Options**. (See **Spell Check Options**, page 241, and **Grammar Check Options**, page 244.)*

1. Place cursor where you want to begin spell/grammar check, or select text to check.

2. Click **Spelling and Grammar** button ⬛ABC✓⬛ in **Standard** toolbar.
   OR
   Click **Tools, Spelling and Grammar** ..... ⬛Alt⬛ + ⬛T⬛,⬛S⬛
   OR
   Press **F7** .... ⬛F7⬛

continued.

3. Select the **Chec_k_ grammar** check box .... K
   if desired, to check both spelling and grammar.

*The **Spelling and Grammar** dialog box displays, with spelling and/or grammar errors appearing in the first window. The title of this window varies, depending on the error. You can edit the errors displayed, and suggested solutions are displayed in the **Suggestions** list box.*

To select a custom dictionary for spell check:

Note: You must first activate a custom dictionary to be able to use it during spell check.

a. Click Options... .... Alt + O

b. Click **Custom dictio_n_ary** ...... Alt + N , ↑ ↓
   and select custom dictionary to use.

Be sure to check the box next to the desired dictionary to activate it during spell check.

c. Click OK .... ↵

To replace proposed error with suggested solution:

a. Click **Sugg_e_stions** list box ... Alt + E , ↑ ↓
   and select desired suggestion.

b. Click _C_hange .... Alt + C
   to replace error with suggested alternative.

OR

Click Change A_ll_ .... Alt + L
   to replace all instances of error with the selected alternative.

continued...

240

SPELL AND GRAMMAR CHECK (CONTINUED)

To change an error directly in the document:

a. Click in document and type change.

b. Click `Resume` .... Alt + S
    in **Spelling and Grammar** dialog box,
    to continue Spell and Grammar check.

To leave error unaltered and continue checking:

Click `Ignore` .... Alt + I

OR

Click `Ignore All` .... Alt + G
to skip all instances of error in rest of document.

OR

Click `Next Sentence` .... Alt + N
to skip all other errors in current sentence
and move to the next sentence containing errors.

To reverse last action:

Click `Undo` .... Alt + U

To add unrecognized word to AutoCorrect list:

Click `AutoCorrect` .... Alt + R
*(See **AUTOCORRECT**, page 225.)*

To add an unrecognized word to dictionary:

Click `Add` .... Alt + A

**To change dictionary to which you want to add
unrecognized words:**

a. Click in **Not in dictionary:** .... Alt + : , ↑ ↓
    and select word to add to dictionary.

continued

b. Click [Options...] .... O

*The **Spelling and Grammar Options** dialog box displays.*

c. Click **Custom dictionary** box .... N , ↑ ↓
and select dictionary to add words to.

d. Click [OK] .... ↵

Note: *See **Spell Check Options**, below, for
information on creating and editing custom
dictionaries.*

**To exit Spelling and Grammar dialog box
without making any changes:**

Click [Cancel] .... Esc

4. Click [Close] .... Esc
to exit **Spelling** dialog box after making changes.

Spell Check Options

*Customizes Word's spell check operation. Also activates
custom or supplemental dictionaries to check words that the
spell checker doesn't recognize, such as technical terms or text
in other languages.*

1. a. Click **Tools**, **Spelling & Grammar** .... Alt + T , S

b. Click [Options...] .... Alt + O

*The **Spelling and Grammar Options** dialog box displays.*

OR

a. Click **Tools**, **Options** .... Alt + T , O

*The **Options** dialog box displays.*

b. Click [Spelling & Grammar]

continued...

242

2. Select from the following **Spelling** options:

- **Check spelling errors as you type** .... `Alt` + `P`
  to have Word automatically check
  spelling as you work.

- **Hide spelling errors in this document** .... `Alt` + `S`
  to prevent Word from marking spelling
  errors found as you work. Deselect this
  option to have Word automatically mark
  spelling errors with a wavy red line that
  appears on screen, but does not print.

Note: This option is only available if you selected
***Check spelling errors as you type**, above.*

- **Always suggest corrections** .... `Alt` + `L`
  to have Word automatically display
  replacement suggestions for misspellings
  when you run a spell check.

- **Suggest from main dictionary only** ...... `Alt` + `M`
  to have Word suggest replacement spellings
  from the main dictionary only. Deselect to
  have Word suggest spellings from all open
  custom dictionaries, in addition to the main one.

- **Ignore words in UPPERCASE** .... `Alt` + `U`

- **Ignore words with numbers** .... `Alt` + `B`

- **Ignore Internet and file Addresses** .... `Alt` + `F`

To create a new custom dictionary:

a. Click `Dictionaries...` .... `Alt` + `D`

b. Click `New...` .... `Alt` + `N`

*The **Create Custom Dictionary** dialog box displays.*

continued.

SPELL CHECK OPTIONS (CONTINUED)

c. Click **File name** box .... **Alt** + **N**, *filename*
   and type file name for new dictionary.

d. Click [Save] .... **Alt** + **S**
   to close **Create Custom Dictionary**
   dialog box.

Note: *Custom dictionaries are stored in the Proof*
folder by default.

e. Add words to custom dictionary during
   Spell check, as desired. *(See SPELL AND
   GRAMMAR CHECK, page 238.)*

To edit a custom dictionary:

a. Click [Dictionaries...] .... **Alt** + **D**

b. Select custom dictionary to edit.

Note: *Do not clear check box next to*
selected dictionary.

c. Click [Edit] .... **Alt** + **E**

The Custom dictionary window displays.

d. Add, delete, or edit words in list.

Note: *If adding words, be sure to press Enter*
after each, so that each word is on a
separate line.

e. Click **File**, **Save** .... **Alt** + **F**, **S**
   OR
   Click **Save** button 🖫 in the **Standard** toolbar.

f. Click **Close** button ✕ in **Custom**
   dictionary window.

continued...

SPELL CHECK OPTIONS (CONTINUED)

To remove custom dictionary:

a. Click `Dictionaries...` .... `Alt` + `D`

b. Select custom dictionary to remove...... `↑` `↓`

c. Click `Remove` .... `Alt` + `R`

d. Click `OK` .... `↵`

To select language for custom dictionary:

a. Click `Dictionaries...` .... `Alt` + `D`

b. Click **Language** box .... `Alt` + `G`, `↑` `↓`
   and select desired language.

c. Click `OK` .... `↵`

Note: *Language spell checking only applies to text that has been formatted in that language. (See **LANGUAGE**, page 230.)*

3. Click `OK` .... `↵`

Grammar Check Options

Use Word's grammar options to specify rules of grammar and writing styles to use. You can use built–in styles, or create your own by customizing an existing style or defining a new one.

1. a. Click **T**ools, **S**pelling & Grammar .... `Alt` + `T`, `S`

   b. Click `Options...` .... `Alt` + `O`

*The **Spelling and Grammar Options** dialog box displays.*

   OR

   a. Click **T**ools, **O**ptions .... `Alt` + `T`, `O`

*The **Options** dialog box displays.*

   b. Click `Spelling & Grammar`

continued.

2. Select from the following grammar options:

- **Check grammar as you type** .... `Alt`+`G`
  to have Word check grammar as you work.

- **Hide grammatical errors in this document** ... `Alt`+`E`
  to prevent Word from marking grammatical
  errors found as you work. Deselect this
  option to have Word automatically mark
  spelling errors with a wavy green line that
  appears on screen, but does not print.

Note: *This option is only available if you selected*
Check grammar errors as you type above.

- **Check grammar with spelling** .... `Alt`+`H`
  to have Word automatically check
  grammar whenever you run spell check.

- **Show readability statistics** .... `Alt`+`R`
  to have Word automatically display the
  Readability statistics dialog box when
  you run a spell/grammar check.

3. Click **Writing style** box........................... `Alt`+`W`
   and select desired style.

   To customize grammar and style rules:

   a. Click [Settings...] .... `Alt`+`T`

   *The **Grammar Settings** dialog box displays.*

   b. Select desired grammar and style rule settings.

   c. Click [OK] ....↵

   To reset default grammar and style rules:

   Click [Reset All] .... `Alt`+`R`

4. Click [OK] ....↵

THESAURUS

1. Select word or phrase for which you want to find a synonym, antonym, or related word.

2. a. Click <u>T</u>ools, <u>L</u>anguage .... `Alt`+`T`,`L`

   b. Click <u>T</u>hesaurus .... `T`

   OR

   Press **Shift+F7** .... `Shift`+`F7`

*The **Thesaurus** dialog box opens, with selected word or phrase appearing in **Looked Up** box. If selected word or phrase is not found, an alphabetical list displays possible alternatives.*

To look up additional meanings for word displayed in Looked Up box:

   a. Click <u>M</u>eanings list box .... `Alt`+`M`,`↑``↓` and select related word to look up.

   b. Click [<u>L</u>ook Up] .... `Alt`+`L`

*The word selected in step a appears in the **Looked Up** box, definitions for that word appear in the **Meanings list** box, and synonyms for it appear in the **Replace with Synonym** list box.*

To look up additional synonyms for a word or phrase:

   a. Click Replace with <u>S</u>ynonym .... `Alt`+`S`,`↑``↓` box and select word to look up synonyms for.

   b. Click [<u>L</u>ook Up] .... `Alt`+`L`

*Word displays a list of synonyms for the selected word in the **Replace with Synonym** box.*

continued

**To look up a word previously looked up
during the current thesaurus session:**

Click **Looked Up** box .... `Alt`+`K`, `↑` `↓`
and select word or phrase to look up.

OR

Click `Previous` .... `Alt`+`P`

**To replace selected word in document with a
word suggested in Thesaurus dialog box:**

a. Click **Replace with Synonym**.... `Alt`+`S`, `↑` `↓`
   box and select replacement word.

b. Click `Replace` .... `Alt`+`R`

WORD COUNT

1. Click **Tools**, **Word Count** .... `Alt`+`T`, `W`

*The **Word Count** dialog box displays with statistics for the
active document.*

2. Click **Include footnotes and endnotes** ... `Alt`+`F`
   if desired, to include footnotes and endnotes
   when compiling document statistics.

3. Click `Close` .... `Esc`
   to exit **Word Count** dialog box.

MAIL OPTIONS
ADDRESS BOOK
Display Insert Address Icon on Standard Toolbar

1. Click **View**, **Toolbars**...................... `Alt`+`V`, `T`

2. Click **Customize**.. `C`

3. Click `Commands`

4. Click the **Categories** list box.....`Alt`+`G`, `↑` `↓`
   and select **Insert**.

5. Click **Commands** list box..........`Alt`+`D`, `↑` `↓`
   and select 📖 Address Book... from list.

6. Click on address book icon 📖 and drag
   it onto the **Standard** toolbar.

Insert Address from Address Book

Inserts names and addresses from address books created with Microsoft Outlook™ 97 or Microsoft Schedule+ 95, or other MAPI–compatible messaging system address lists.

> Note: This option is also available in some dialog boxes and wizards.

1. Place cursor in document where you want to insert entry from your address book.

2. Click drop–down arrow on **Insert Address** button 📖 ▾
   in the **Standard** toolbar, and select an address to insert from the list of recently used addresses.

continued.

INSERT ADDRESS FROM ADDRESS BOOK (CONTINUED)

OR

Click the **Insert Address** button 📖 in the **Standard** toolbar.

*Note: The **Choose Profile** dialog box may display. Select the user profile you want to use and click **OK**.*

*The **Select Name** dialog displays.*

3. Click **Show names from the** ..... `Alt`+`S`, `↑` `↓` box and select address book containing address to insert.

4. Click **Type Name or Select** .... `Alt`+`Y`, *name* **from List** box and type desired name.

    To create new address book entry:

    Click `New...` .... `Alt`+`N`

    To display properties for selected address book entry:

    Click `Properties...` .... `Alt`+`P`

5. Click `OK` .... `↵`

*The **Select Name** dialog box closes, and selected address is inserted in document.*

ENVELOPES AND LABELS

*Note: To print envelopes using a file containing names and addresses, use **MAIL MERGE** procedures, page 257.*

Create Envelope

1. Select delivery address contained in document. If current document does not contain address to print, leave cursor as flashing insertion point.

2. Click **T**ools, **E**nvelopes and Labels ..... `Alt`+`T`,`E`

*The **Envelopes and Labels** dialog box displays.*

3. Click `Envelopes` .... `Alt`+`E`

4. Click **D**elivery Address box ..... `Alt`+`D`, *address* and type delivery address or make desired edits to address selected in step **1**.

   OR

   To select an address from your Address Book:

   a. Click **Insert Address** button 📖

   b. Follow procedures 3–5 under **Insert Address from Address Book**, page 248.

   OR

   Click drop–down arrow next to **Address** button 📖▼ and select address from list of recently used addresses.

5. Click **R**eturn Address list box .. `Alt`+`R`, *address* and type return address or make desired changes to default address.

   *Note: Default return address is the mailing address in **User Information** tab of **Options** dialog box. (see **USER INFORMATION**, page 37.)*

   OR

   To omit return address from envelope:

   Select **O**mit check box .... `Alt`+`M`

continued.

251

To set envelope options:

a. Click [**Options...**] .... `Alt`+`O`

*The **Envelope Options** dialog box displays.*

b. Click [Envelope Options] .... `Alt`+`E`

c. Click **Envelope size** box ...... `Alt`+`S`, `↑` `↓`
   and select an envelope size.

d. Select desired **If Mailed in the USA** options:

   • **Delivery Point barcode**.............. `Alt`+`B`

   • **FIM–A Courtesy Reply Mail**............ `Alt`+`A`

*Note: This option is only available when you
          select **Delivery Point Bar Code** above.*

e. Click [**Font...**] .... `Alt`+`F`
   to change delivery address font.

   OR

   Click [**Font...**] .... `Alt`+`O`
   to change return address font.

*The **Envelope Address** or **Envelope Return Address**
dialog box displays.*

f. Change font as desired. *(See **Font**, page 101.)*

g. Click **From left** box.............. `Alt`+`L`, *number*
   and type distance to place
   between delivery address and
   left edge of envelope (default is **Auto**).

   OR

continued...

CREATE ENVELOPE (CONTINUED)

Click **From top** box .... `Alt`+`T`, *number*
and type distance to place
between delivery address and top
edge of envelope (default is **Auto**).

h. Click **From left** box .... `Alt`+`M`, *number*
and type distance to place
between return address and left
edge of envelope (default is **Auto**).

OR

Click **From top** box .... `Alt`+`R`, *number*
and type distance to place
between return address and top
edge of envelope (default is **Auto**).

i. Click [OK] .... `↵`

To set printing options:

a. Click [Options...] .... `Alt`+`O`

*The **Envelope Options** dialog box displays.*

b. Click [Printing Options] .... `Alt`+`P`

c. Select an envelope placement option:

- **Face up** .... `Alt`+`U`

- **Face down** .... `Alt`+`D`

d. Select **Clockwise rotation** .... `Alt`+`C`
check box, if desired, to reverse direction
of envelope when you insert it in printer.

e. Click desired envelope orientation from
images displayed under **Feed Method**.

continued..

f. Click **Feed from** box .... `Alt`+`F`, `↑` `↓`
and select printer tray to feed
envelopes into.

g. Click [**OK**] .... `↵`

OR

Click [**Reset**] .... `Alt`+`R`
to return Printing Options to original settings
proposed by Word.

6. Click [**Print**] .... `Alt`+`P`

OR

Click [**Add to Document**] .... `Alt`+`A`

Notes: *If you add an envelope to a document, Word*
inserts a section break, which contains
envelope formatting, before or after it.

If changes were made to return address, a
prompt displays asking if new return
address is to be saved as default.

Create Labels

Note: *To print mailing labels using a file*
containing names and addresses, use
***MAIL MERGE** procedures, page 257.*

1. Select address contained in current document.
If document does not contain address to print,
leave cursor as flashing cursor.

2. Click **Tools**, **Envelopes and Labels** ..... `Alt`+`T`, `E`

*The **Envelopes and Labels** dialog box displays.*

3. Click [Labels] .... `Alt`+`L`

continued...

254

4. Click **Address** box................... Alt + A , *address*
   and type address, or edit address
   selected in step 1.

   **To use name and address stored in User
   Information tab of Options dialog box:**

   Note: See **USER INFORMATON**, *page 37.*

   Click **Use return address**........................ Alt + R

   To select an address from your Address Book:

   a. Click **Insert Address** button 📖

   b. Follow procedures 3–5 under **Insert
      Address from Address Book**, page 248.

   OR

   Click drop–down arrow next to **Address** button 📖▼
   and select address from list of recently used addresses.

5. Click **Delivery Point barcode**................... Alt + B
   if desired, to print POSTNET (Postal
   Numeric Encoding Technique) bar code.

6. Click **Full page of the same label** .... Alt + F
   to print address on every label on sheet.

   OR

   a. Click **Single label**............................. Alt + N
      to print address on a single label on sheet.

   b. Click **Row**............................ Alt + W , *number*
      and type the number of the row
      containing label to print address on.

   c. Click **Column** .... Alt + C , *number*
      and type number of column
      containing label to print address on.

continued.

To set label options:

a. Click `Options...` .... `Alt` + `O`

*The **Label Options** dialog box displays.*

b. Click **Dot matrix** .... `Alt` + `M`

OR

- Click **Laser and ink jet**............... `Alt` + `L`

- Click **Tray** box .... `Alt` + `T` , `↑` `↓`
  and select printer tray.

c. Click **Label Products** box .... `Alt` + `P` , `↑` `↓`
   and select label type to use.

d. Click **Product number**.......... `Alt` + `U` , `↑` `↓`
   box and select product number
   for labels you plan to use.

Note: If desired label isn't listed, click
   `New Label...` *and create custom label.*

e. Click `Details...` .... `Alt` + `D`
   to set more detailed label options.

*The **Label Information** dialog box displays. The title of the
dialog box changes to reflect the selected type of label.*

*Note: Various options in **Label Information** dialog
   box are not available for all label types.*

f. Click **Top margin** box .... `Alt` + `T` , *number*
   and type distance between top
   edge of label and first line of text.

g. Click **Side margin** box......... `Alt` + `S` , *number*
   and type distance between
   left edge of label and text.

continued...

256

CREATE LABEL (CONTINUED)

h. Click **Vertical pitch** .... `Alt`+`V`, *number*
   and type distance between top
   of one label and top of label below.

i. Click **Horizontal pitch** .... `Alt`+`O`, *number*
   and type distance between left
   edge of label and left edge of
   label next to it.

j. Click **Label height** .... `Alt`+`E`, *number*
   and type distance between top
   and bottom edges of label.

k. Click **Label width**................ `Alt`+`W`, *number*
   and type distance between left
   and right edges of label.

l. Click **Number across** .... `Alt`+`A`, *number*
   and type number of labels per
   row on your sheet of labels.

m. Click **Number down** .... `Alt`+`D`, *number*
   and type number of labels per
   column on your sheet of labels.

n. Click **Page size** .... `Alt`+`P`, *number*
   and type dimensions of label sheet.

o. Click [**OK**] .... `↵`

7. Click [**Print**] ....`Alt`+`P`
   OR
   Click [**New Document**] ....`Alt`+`D`

   Note: *This option is unavailable if **Single Label**
   was selected in previous step.*

MAIL MERGE

*A mail merge combines the contents of a **main document** and a **data source**. A main document contains information that does not change, such as the body of a form letter. A data source contains information, known as **records**, that vary with each merged document (e.g., names and addresses).*

*Creating a mail merge involves several steps: creating the main document, creating the data source, inserting merge fields into the main document, and then merging the two completed documents together. The **Mail Merge Helper** is a Word feature designed to assist in this process.*

*The following procedures describe how to set up a basic mail merge. (See your Word documentation, or refer to online **Help** for information on advanced options and techniques.)*

Mail Merge Toolbar

*After creating a mail merge main document, the **Mail Merge** toolbar displays. The **Mail Merge** toolbar buttons and their associated commands are as follows:*

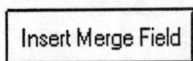

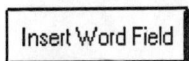

Insert Merge Field	*Inserts a merge field into document at the location of the cursor.*
Insert Word Field	*Inserts a Word field into document at the location of the cursor.*
«» ABC	***View Merged Data** button. Toggles between displaying merge fields and records from the data source.*
◀	***First Record** button. Displays how first record in attached data source appears when merged with main document.*
◀	***Previous Record** button. Displays how the previous record in the attached data source appears when merged with the main document.*

continued...

258

Go To Record box. Selects a specific record to display from attached data source when merged with the main document.

Next Record button. Displays how next record in attached data source appears when merged with main document.

Last Record button. Displays how last record in attached data source appears when merged with main document.

Mail Merge Helper button. Displays Mail Merge Helper dialog box.

Check for Errors button. Checks the mail merge for errors.

Merge to New Document button. Automatically merges main document and data source to new document.

Merge to Printer button. Merges main document and data source to printer.

Mail Merge button. Displays Merge dialog box, used for selecting specific records to merge, query options, and other choices when merging main document and data source.

Find Record button. Searches for specific record in attached data source.

Edit Data Source button. Displays Data Form dialog box, used for managing records in data source.

Mail Merge Keyboard Shortcuts

Selects various mail merge commands using keyboard shortcuts. After creating the main document and data source using the procedures described in the following pages, you can select any of the following keystrokes:

Command:	Press:
Preview mail merge	Shift + Alt + K
Merge document..............................	Shift + Alt + N
Print merged document	Shift + Alt + M
Edit mail merge..............................	Shift + Alt + E
data document	
Insert merge field...........................	Shift + Alt + F

Set Up Main Document

Note: This command is also used to restore a
         mail merge main document to a normal
         Word document.

1 Open document to use as main document,
   or create new document to use. *(See **OPEN FILE**,
   page 52, and **CREATE NEW FILE**, page 38.)*

2. Click **T**ools, Mail Me**r**ge................   Alt + T , R

*The **Mail Merge Helper** dialog box displays.*

3. Click [**C**reate ▼] ....   Alt + C

4. Select type of merge document to set up from the
    following options:

    • Form **L**etters   L

    • **M**ailing Labels ....   M

    • **E**nvelopes ....   E

continued...

260

SET UP MAIN DOCUMENT (CONTINUED)

- **C**atalog .... $\boxed{\text{C}}$

- Restore to **N**ormal Word Document .... $\boxed{\text{N}}$

Note: *This option is only available if the active document is a mail merge main document.*

A prompt displays, asking if you want to use the active window or create a new document to use as the mail merge main document.

5. Click [**Active Window**] .... $\boxed{\text{Alt}}+\boxed{\text{A}}$

   to use displayed document as main document.

   OR

   Click [**New Main Document**] .... $\boxed{\text{Alt}}+\boxed{\text{N}}$

*The **Mail Merge Helper** dialog box redisplays.*

6. Click [Edit ▼] .... $\boxed{\text{Alt}}+\boxed{\text{E}}, \boxed{\text{↵}}$

Mail merge main document opens.

7. Type generic text of main document that will remain the same for all versions.

8. Follow steps for **Attach Data Source**, below, to insert personalized name and address information.

Attach Data Source

Creates a new data source or opens an existing data source. This command also allows you to specify a separate header row file for the data source. A header row is the top row in a data source table that contains merge fields, which identify the various types of information contained in each column of the data source.

OPEN EXISTING DATA SOURCE

1. Follow procedures in **Set Up Main Document**, page 259.

2. Click **Tools, Mail Merge**.................. `Alt`+`T`,`R`

*The **Mail Merge Helper** dialog box displays.*

3. Click [**Get Data** ▼] .... `Alt`+`G`,`O`
   and select **Open Data Source**.

   Note: *This option is only available if active file is set
            up as mail merge main document.*

*The **Open Data Source** dialog box opens.*

4. Click **Files of type** box...... `Alt`+`T`,`↑`,`↓`,`↵`
   if desired, to display other
   source file types (e.g., Microsoft
   Access files, Excel files, etc.).

   Note: *Word will automatically translate
            compatible non-Word files.*

5. Open file containing desired data.
   *(See **OPEN FILE**, page 52.)*

USE ADDRESS BOOK AS DATA SOURCE

1. Follow procedures in **Set Up Main Document**, page 259.

2. Click **Tools, Mail Merge**.................. `Alt`+`T`,`R`

*The **Mail Merge Helper** dialog box displays.*

3. Click [**Get Data** ▼] .... `Alt`+`G`,`A`
   and select **Use Address Book**.

   Note: *This option is available only if active file is
            set up as a mail merge main document.*

*The **Use Address Book** dialog box displays.*

4. Click **Choose Address Book** ..... `Alt`+`C`,`↑`,`↓`
   box and select an address book.

continued...

262

USE ADDRESS BOOK AS DATA SOURCE (CONTINUED)

*Address books created with Microsoft Exchange Server,
Microsoft Outlook, Schedule+ 2.0 contact lists, or other MAPI–
compatible messaging system address lists display on screen.*

5. Click [OK] .... ⏎

CREATE DATA SOURCE

1. Follow procedures in **Set Up Main Document**, page 259.

2. Click **Tools, Mail Merge** .... `Alt`+`T`,`R`

*The **Mail Merge Helper** dialog box displays.*

3. Click [**Get Data ▼**] .... `Alt`+`G`,`C`
    and select **Create Data Source.**

> Notes: This option is only available if active file is
> set up as mail merge main document.
>
> A mail merge data source contains columns
> of data labeled by field names, which appear
> in the header row. Commonly used field
> names are listed in **Field names in header
> row** list box. You can add, remove, or
> rearrange these default names to create
> custom header row.
>
> Header row must contain same number of
> field names as there are field columns in
> data source.

*The **Create Data Source** dialog box displays.*

To add a custom field name to header row list:

a. Click **Field name** box...... `Alt`+`F`, *field name*
    and type new field name.

b. Click [**Add Field Name ▶▶**] .... `Alt`+`A`

continued.

To remove a field name from header row list:

a. Click **Field names in**.............. `Alt` + `N`, `↑` `↓`
   header row list box and select
   field name to remove.

b. Click | **Remove Field Name** | .... `Alt` + `R`

To reorder field names in header row list:

a. Click **Field names in**.............. `Alt` + `N`, `↑` `↓`
   header row list box and select
   field name to move.

b. Click **Move Up** or **Move Down** buttons `↑` `↓`

4. Click | **OK** | .... `↵`

*The **Save As** dialog box displays.*

5. Save new data source. *(See **SAVE FILE**, page 54.)*

*A prompt displays, telling you that there is no data in your new
data source, and asking whether you want to edit the data
source to add data records to it, or edit the main document, to
add merge fields to it.*

6. Click | Edit Data Source | .... `Alt` + `D`

*The **Data Form** dialog box displays.*

> Note: Field names selected in step 3 appear in
>   left–hand column of dialog box, with blank
>   text boxes across from them, where data
>   can be typed.

To add new records to data source:

a. Press **Tab** or **Shift+Tab** ...... `Tab` or `Shift` + `Tab`
   to move between fields.

continued..

264

    b. Type information... *text*
       into selected field name boxes.

    Note: Do not type spaces in field text boxes.

    c. Click [**A̲dd New**] .... `Alt`+`A`

    d. Repeat steps a–c to add additional records.

To move between records:

Click one of the following buttons:

- **Next record**....................................... `▶`

- **Previous record** .... `◀`

- **First record**.. `I◀`

- **Last record** .... `▶I`

OR

    a. Click **R̲ecord** box .... `Alt`+`R`, *number*
       and type desired record number.

    b. Press **ENTER**.. `⏎`

7. For each record to modify, select one of the
    following options:

- Click [**D̲elete**] .... `Alt`+`D`
    to remove record from data source.

- Click [**Re̲store**] .... `Alt`+`S`
    to restore record to its original contents.

- Click [**F̲ind...**] .... `Alt`+`F`
    to search data source for specified information.

continued...

CREATE DATA SOURCE (CONTINUED)

- Click [**View Source**] .... `Alt` + `V`
  to view data source file in table form.

Note: *Viewing the data source file allows you to*
       edit data records using Database toolbar.

8. Click [**OK**] .... `↵`

Word returns to main document. When you close main
document, you will be prompted to save changes to data source.

To save data source changes before returning to
the main document:

a. Click [**View Source**] .... `Alt` + `V`

b. Click **File, Save** .... `Alt` + `F` , `S`

Insert Merge Fields into Main Document

INSERT MERGE FIELD INTO MAIN DOCUMENT USING MENU

1. Place cursor in mail merge main document
   where you want to insert merge field.

2. Press **Shift+Alt+F** .... `Shift` + `Alt` + `F`

The Insert Merge Field dialog box displays.

3. Click **Mail merge fields** .... `Alt` + `M` , `↑` `↓`
   box and select merge field to insert.

4. Click **Word fields** box.............. `Alt` + `W` , `↑` `↓`
   and select Word field to insert.

5. Repeat steps 1–4 to insert additional merge fields.

6. Click [**OK**] .... `↵`

INSERT MERGE FIELD USING TOOLBAR

1. Place cursor in mail merge main document where you want to insert merge field.

2. a. Click **Insert Merge Field** button `Insert Merge Field` in Mail Merge toolbar.

   b. Select desired merge field.....................↑↓

   To insert a Word field:

   a. Click **Insert Word Field** button `Insert Word Field` in **Mail Merge** toolbar.

   b. Select desired Word field.....................↑↓

3. Repeat steps 1–2 to insert additional merge fields.

Merge Main Document and Data Source

*Merges the main document and attached data source with the **Tools**, **Mail Merge** command. This command allows you to select query options and various other choices.*

1. Click **Mail Merge** button in **Mail Merge** toolbar.
   OR
   a. Click **Tools, Mail Merge** .... Alt + T , R

   *The **Mail Merge Helper** dialog box displays.*

   b. Click `Merge...` .... Alt + M

   *The **Merge** dialog box displays.*

2. Click **Merge To** box.................. Alt + R , ↑↓ and select where to send output (**New Document** or **Printer**).

3. Click **All** .... Alt + A to merge all records in data source.

continued.

MERGE MAIN DOCUMENT & DATA SOURCE (CONTINUED)
OR

a. Click **F**rom box .... `Alt`+`F`, *number*
and type number of first
record in range to merge.

b. Click **T**o box......................... `Alt`+`T`, *number*
and type number of last
record in range to merge.

4. Select a **When Merging Records** option:

- **D**on't print blank lines when .... `Alt`+`D`
data fields are empty

- **P**rint blank lines when .... `Alt`+`P`
data fields are empty

5. Click **Check Errors...** .... `Alt`+`E`

*The **Checking and Reporting Errors** dialog box displays.*

6. Select error checking option:

- **S**imulate the merge and report .... `Alt`+`S`
errors in a new document

- **C**omplete the merge, pausing to .... `Alt`+`C`
report each error as it occurs

- Complete the **m**erge without pausing...... `Alt`+`M`
and report errors in a new document

7. Click **OK** .... `↵`

*The **Merge** dialog box redisplays.*

To select query options for mail merge:

a. Click **Query Options...** .... `Alt`+`Q`

b. Click **Filter Records** .... `Alt`+`F`

continued...

268

MERGE MAIN DOCUMENT & DATA SOURCE (CONTINUED)

c. Click **Field** box.............................. ⬆️⬇️,↵
and select data field for Word to search
in each data record, comparing its contents
to criteria designated in **Compare to** box.

d. Click the **Comparison** box.............. ⬆️⬇️,↵
and select an operator to compare by.

e. Click the **Compare to** box ....*text/number*
and type text/number to compare
designated data field in each data record.

f. Click **And** or **Or**, and repeat steps c–e, above, to
filter data records by multiple search criteria.

g. Click **Clear All**, if desired, to delete filter criteria
and select all data records in data source.

h. Click `Sort Records` .... Alt + O

i. Click **Sort by** box.......... Alt + S, ⬆️⬇️,↵
and select field to sort by.

j. Click **Then by** box .... Alt + T, ⬆️⬇️,↵
and select second field to sort by.

k. Click **Then by** box .... Alt + B, ⬆️⬇️,↵
and select third field to sort by.

l. Click a sort order for each selected sort field:

- **Ascending**
  to place entries with lowest numbers, or letters closest
  to the beginning of alphabet, at top of sorted list.

- **Descending**
  to place entries with highest numbers, or letters
  closest to end of alphabet, at top of sorted list.

8. Click `Merge...` .... ↵

Index

A

B

270

Index

Index   271

272

Index

Index

273

Index

275

Index

278   Index